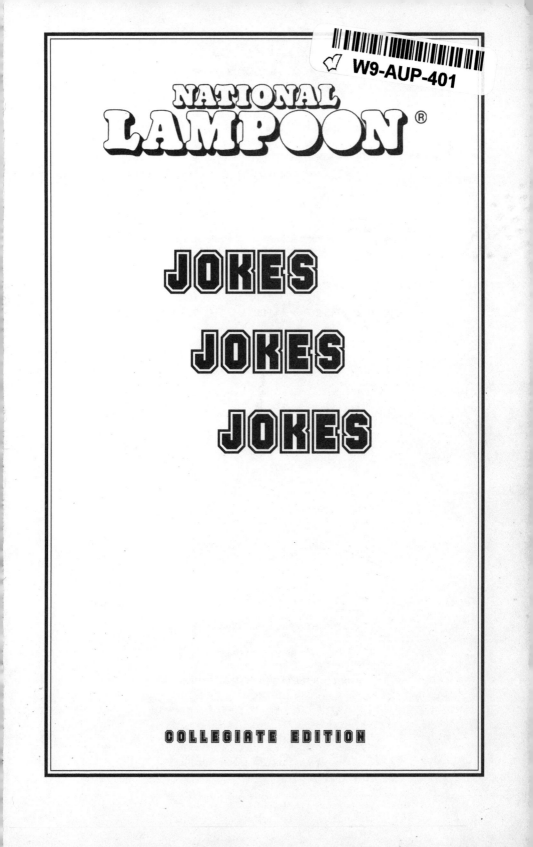

NATIONAL LAMPOON®

JOKES JOKES JOKES

COLLEGIATE EDITION

Published by National Lampoon Press

National Lampoon, Inc. • 10850 Wilshire Blvd., Suite 1000 • Los Angeles • CA 90024 • USA • AMEX:NLN

NATIONAL LAMPOON, NATIONAL LAMPOON PRESS and colophon are trademarks of National Lampoon

National lampoon, jokes jokes jokes, the collegiate edition / by Steve Ochs
with Joke Analysis by Mason Brown. -- 1st ed.

p. cm.

ISBN 0-9778718-2-7   - $11.95 U.S.   - $15.95 Canada

Book Design and Production by
JK NAUGHTON

Cover Design by
MoDMaN

PRINTED IN THE UNITED STATES OF AMERICA

1   3   5   7   9   10   8   6   4   2

JULY 2006

WWW.NATIONALLAMPOON.COM

Contents

Introduction

Throughout my fourteen year run as a stand up comic I never used my real name; I have many enemies.

During my travels to comedy clubs and colleges throughout the land, I would be repeatedly cornered by audience members who wanted to share a joke with me. I don't want to slam comedy audiences overall, because on the whole, they're pretty great. But the people who would pin me down were usually haphazardly-shaved white guys with hypertension and an exhale thick with the salami smell of a rotting tooth. Not a job perk. "I'll bet you already know this one," they would speculate, making the act of telling me the joke an even bigger waste of time. Great, we get to spend a special moment together where I learn about your oral hygiene and you force a joke you believe I already know into the ear I'm straining toward you only because I need to turn my olfactory apparatus as far away from you as my twisting neck can take it.

I came to hate the joke. Though it was impossible to block out all of them, I was able to push them so far back into my mind that it would have taken regression hypnosis to find them.

Then, years after I had left stand up and turned to writing, and under a new assumed name – yeah, like I came out of a decade and half of stand up with *fewer* enemies! – I found myself working with your friends at the venerable *National Lampoon*. As a serious, long time fan of the 'Poon, I couldn't resist getting my name on a book under that legendary logo, even if it meant a confrontation with the jokes I had suppressed so diligently.

The idea was simple; *National Lampoon's Jokes, Jokes Jokes Collegiate Edition* would be the "Mr. Boston's" of sophomoric joke telling. The book would cater to the humor needs of young men unable to meet them for themselves.

This mini-encyclopedia of funny would provide a joke where and when it was needed. Further, the book would insure that there are enough jokes on a given topic to allow a performance to last. Kind of a kooky Viagra for the man who can't achieve or maintain elations.

Of course, I thought that the publishers might prefer a writer who actually went to college . . . or high school for that matter. But, no. They felt that the experience of college would have likely left me weak-willed and neurotic. They wanted the kind of daring only found in those who have quit big, life-altering things to their own detriment. Nobody quits like me. I can't believe I actually finished the book.

Anyway, I began researching. I must have been at it for 70 or 80 seconds and, boom, there they were; jokes. Deep in my mind, in the e-mails of friends, and pretty much everywhere else if you're looking: jokes. Jokes about animal dick, farmer dick, priest dick and, yes, even woman dick. Some vaginas, to be sure, but jokes are a man's world.

As you must have seen marching up Main Street, I started laughing. Jokes, I was learning, are not so bad when you can experience them voluntarily. The further I went the more jokes I liked. I even started liking aspects of jokes I had never noticed. For example, did you ever consider how compelling the first lines could be on their own?

A SHORT LIST OF COMPELLING FIRST LINES

Q: What's 40 feet long, and smells like piss?

Two fleas from Detroit had an agreement.

Once upon a time there was this sperm called Brian

A gynecologist was getting sick of his job

This big, nasty, sweaty woman . . .

Jake, an older fellow, joins a nudist colony

A man wakes up one morning to find a gorilla on his roof.

After attending the funeral of a mouse killed while playing football . . .

There was a midget who complained to his buddy that his testicles ached all the time.

And, there are tons of punchlines that could check their set ups at the gate and fly alone.

A BRIEF COLLECTION OF FLY-ALONE PUNCHLINES

"No, because you are ugly."

"I just came in my pants!"

"If the gorilla knocks me off the roof, shoot the dog!"

"Play it? If I can figure out how to get it's pajamas off, I'm going to fuck it."

"He's happy now. But just wait until we take the pacifier out of his ass."

"Why do you ask, Two Dogs Fucking?"

"I see," says the manager, "and is this cunt giving you a hard time?"

"If she finds her way home, don't fuck her."

"He didn't hang himself. I put him there to dry."

"I get erections about once a month, but I fart, like, 18 times a day!"

So, here they are; an ersatz personality for the lame, a treasure trove of verse for the young man on the go who is gloriously unburdened by a funny bone. Even if you're a cut up, this selection should amuse or at least provide an opportunity to read something that looks like a text book but actually makes sense to you.

But I should offer an apology to those still performing stand up at clubs and colleges across the country. This book could very well nurture a new generation of beer-sweating, nacho crumb-adorned audience members who will inevitably corner you and belch the contents into your ear. For this, I am deeply sorry.

—*Steve Ochs*

HBEV 411
HOSPITALITY BEVERAGES

Course:	HBEV 411 Hospitality Beverages
Semester:	Summer of odd years
Credits:	3
Restrictions:	Open only to seniors or graduate students in the Hospitality Business major and Art History majors who will graduate with no marketable skills.
Description:	Evaluation and selection of hospitality beverages. Geographical origins of beverages, beverage consumption, beverage re-assignment (vomiting), matching beverages with food, health and select uses of beverages for social considerations including inhabitation reduction and favorable memory lapse.
Dates:	SUMMER - Open

You know, when you're actually in a bar, a lot of things that shouldn't really be that funny, are. You've probably had a couple, you're loose and goofy and laughing is easy. If you're the kind of person who can't come up with anything funny enough to make drunks laugh, 1. That's terribly, terribly sad and 2. Good thing you picked up this book! The jokes below should put you into the conversation with class-A stuff. That is, unless you've actually brought this book to the bar with you, in which case there are already people laughing at you, so the jokes aren't necessary.

—*Steve*

A drunken man walks into a biker bar, sits down at the bar and orders a drink. Looking around, he sees three men sitting at a corner table. He gets up, staggers to the table, leans over, looks the biggest, meanest, biker in the face and says, "I went by your grandma's house today, and I saw her in the hallway buck naked. Man, she is one fine-looking woman!"

The biker looks at him and doesn't say a word. His buddies are confused, because he is one bad biker and would fight at the drop of a hat.

The drunk leans on the table again and says, "I got it on with your grandma and she is good, the best I ever had!"

The biker's buddies are starting to get really mad, but the biker still says nothing.

The drunk leans on the table one more time and says, "I'll tell you something else, boy, your grandma liked it!"

At this point the biker stands up, takes the drunk by the shoulders, looks him square in the eyes and says, "Grandpa. Go home, you're drunk."

* * * *

This big, nasty, sweaty woman, wearing a sleeveless sundress, walks into a bar. She raises her right arm, revealing a big hairy armpit, as she points to all the people sitting at the bar and asks, "What man out there will buy a lady a drink?"

The whole bar goes dead silent, as the patrons try to ignore her. At the end of the bar, a skinny little drunk slams his hand on the bar and says, "Bartender! I want to buy that ballerina a drink!"

The bartender pours the drink and the woman chugs it down. After she's had the drink, she turns again to the patrons and points around at all of them, again revealing her hairy armpit, saying, "What man out there will buy a lady a drink?"

Once again, the little drunk slaps his hand down on the bar and says, "Bartender! I'd like to buy the ballerina another drink!"

After serving the lady her second drink, the bartender approaches the little drunk and states, "It's your business if you want to buy the lady a drink, but why do you call her a ballerina?"

The drunk replies, "Sir! In my eyes, any woman who can lift her leg up that high has got to be a ballerina!"

* * * *

Ben, a local fisherman, went into his favorite bar and ordered six double vodkas. Bob, the bartender said, "Wow! You must have had a bad day."

"Yeah," said Ben, "I just found out my older brother is gay."

The next day Ben showed up and again ordered six double vodkas. Bob said, "What, more problems?"

"Damn right! I just found out my younger brother is gay."

The third day, the he cheerfully orders a bottle of champagne.

"Hey, did you finally find out someone in your family likes women?" asked Bob.

"Yeah," smiled Ben, "my wife!"

* * * *

X

A guy and a girl meet at a bar. They get along so well that they decide to go to the girl's place.

A few drinks later, the guy takes off his shirt and then washes his hands. He then takes off his pants and washes his hands. The girl watches him and says, "You must be a dentist."

The guy, surprised, says, "Yes, how did you figure that out?"

The girl says, "Easy, you keep washing your hands."

One thing led to another and they make love. After they were done, the girl says, "You must be a great dentist."

The guy, now with a boosted ego says, "Yes, I sure am a great dentist. How did you figure that out?"

The girl says, "Easy, I didn't feel a thing."

* * * *

Four friends, who hadn't seen each other in thirty years, reunited at a bar. After several drinks, one of the men had to use the rest room. Those who remained talked about their kids.

The first guy said, "My son is my pride and joy. He started working at a successful company at the bottom of the barrel. He studied Economics and Business Administration and soon began to climb the corporate ladder, and now he is the president of the company. He became so rich that he gave his best friend a top-of-the-line Mercedes for his birthday."

The second guy said, "Darn, that's really terrific! My son is also my pride and joy. He started working for a big airline, and then went to flight school to become a pilot. Eventually, he became a partner in the company, where he owns the majority of its assets. And no, he's so rich that he gave his best friend a brand new jet for his birthday."

The third man said, "Well, that's terrific! My son studied in the best universities and became an engineer. Then, he started his own construction company and is now a multimillionaire. He also gave away something very nice and expensive to his best friend for his birthday, a 30,000 square foot mansion."

The three friends congratulated each other just as the fourth returned from the restroom and asked "What are all the congratulations for?"

One of the three said, "We were talking about the pride we feel for the successes of our sons. What about your son?"

The fourth man replied, "My son is gay and makes a living dancing as a stripper at a nightclub."

The three friends said, "What a shame. What a disappointment."

The fourth man replied, "No, I'm not ashamed. He's my son and I love him. And he hasn't done too bad either. His birthday was two weeks ago, and he received a Mercedes, a jet and a beautiful 30,000 square foot mansion!"

* * * *

Two men were sitting next to each other at a bar. After a while, one guy looks at the other and says, "I can't help but think, from listening to you, that you're from Ireland" The other guy responds proudly,

"Yes, I am!"

The first guy says, "So am I! And where about from Ireland might you be?"

The other guy answers, "I'm from Dublin, I am."

The first guy responds, "Sure and begora, and so am I! And what street did you live on in Dublin?"

The other guy says, "A lovely little area it was, I lived on McCleary Street in the old central part of town."

The first guy says, "Faith and it's a small world, so did I! So did I!! And to what school would you have been going?"

The other guy answers, "Well now, I went to St. Mary's of course."

The first guy gets excited and says, "And so did I! Hey, what year did you graduate?"

The other guy answers, "Well, now, let's see, I graduated in 1964."

The first guy exclaims, "The good Lord must be smiling down upon us! I can hardly believe our good luck at winding up in the same bar tonight. Can you believe it?!! I graduated from St. Mary's in 1964 my own self."

About this time, Vicky walks into the bar, sits down, and orders a beer. Brian, the bartender, walks over to Vicky and mutters, "It's going to be a long night tonight."

Vicky asks, "Why do you say that, Brian?"

"The Murphy twins are drunk again!"

* * * *

A guy walked into a bar and ordered a triple scotch. The bartender poured him the drink and the guy drank it down in one gulp. "Wow," said the bartender. "Something bad musta happened to you."

"I came home early today," answered the guy. "I went up to the bedroom, and there was my wife having sex with my best friend."

The bartender poured the dude another triple shot. "This one is on the house."

The guy gulped it down once again. The bartender asked, "Did you say anything to your wife?"

The guy answered, "Yeah, I walked up to her and told her we were though. 'Pack your bags and get out!' I told her."

"What about your friend?" asked the bartender.

"I looked him straight in the eyes and said, 'Bad dog!!'"

* * * *

John O'Reilly hoisted his beer and said, "Here's to spending the rest of me life between the legs of me wife!" That won him the top prize at the pub for the best toast of the night!

He went home and told his wife, Mary, "I won the prize for the best toast of the night." She said, "Aye, did ye now? And what was your toast?"

John said, "Here's to spending the rest of me life, sitting in church beside me wife."

"Oh, that is very nice indeed, John!" Mary said.

The next day, Mary ran into one of John's drinking buddies on the street corner. The man chuckled leeringly and said, "John won the prize the other night at the pub with a toast about you, Mary."

She said, "Aye, he told me, and I was a bit surprised meself. You know, he's only been there twice in the last four years. Once he fell asleep, and the other time I had to pull him by the ears to make him come."

* * * *

An American businessman was in Japan hanging out in a local bar. Lonely, he hired a hooker and proceeded to go at it all night with her. She kept screaming "Fugifoo! Fugifoo!" which the guy took to be pleasurable.

The next day, he was golfing with his Japanese counterparts and he got a beautiful 340 yard shot and just 50 yards from the pin. Wanting to impress the clients, he said, "Fugifoo!"

The Japanese clients looked confused and said. "What are you talking about? That's the right hole."

* * * *

It was opening night at the Copacabana Nightclub and the Amazing Claude was topping the bill. People came from miles around to see the famed hypnotist do his stuff. As Claude took to the stage, he announced, "Unlike most stage hypnotists who invite two or three people up onto the stage to be put into a trance, I intend to hypnotize each and every member of the audience."

The excitement was almost electric as Claude withdrew a beautiful antique pocket watch from his coat. "I want you each to keep your eye on this antique watch. It's a very special watch. It's been in my family for six generations."

He began to swing the watch gently back and forth while quietly chanting "Watch the watch, watch the watch, watch the watch...."

The crowd became mesmerized as the watch swayed back and forth, light gleaming off its polished surface. Hundreds of pairs of eyes followed the swaying watch, until suddenly it slipped from the hypnotist's fingers and fell to the floor, breaking into a hundred pieces. "Shit!" said the hypnotist.

It took three weeks to clean up the place!

* * * *

A guy walks into a bar and sees a sign hanging over the bar which reads:

Cheese Sandwich: $1.50 Hand Job: $10.00

He checks his wallet for the necessary payment, then he walks up to the bar and beckons to one of the exceptionally attractive blondes serving drinks to an eager-looking group of men. "Yes?" she inquires, with a knowing smile, "can I help you?"

"Yep, I was wondering," whispers the man, "are you the one who gives the hand jobs?"

"Yes," she purrs, "I am."

Replies the man, "Well, then, wash your hands because I want a cheese sandwich!"

****

A drunk gets up from the bar and heads for the bathroom. A few minutes later, a loud, blood curdling scream is heard from the bathroom. A few minutes after that, another loud scream reverberates through the bar.

The bartender goes into the bathroom to investigate why the drunk is screaming. "What's all the screaming about in there? You're scaring the customers!"

"I'm just sitting here on the toilet and every time I try to flush, something comes up and squeezes the hell out of my testicles."

With that, the bartender opens the door, looks in and says, "You idiot! You're sitting on the mop bucket!"

****

A guy sees a sign outside a bar that says "Piano Player Wanted," so he goes in to apply. The bartender, who is desperate for a player, asks the man to play him something. The man sits down and plays some of the most beautiful music the bartender's ever heard.

"That was amazing," exclaims the bartender. "What was that called?"

"That was something I like to call 'A Weasel Ate My Genitals.'"

"Oh. You know anything else?"

The guy plays another amazingly gorgeous piece. Impressed, the bartender applauds and asks what that one was called.

"It's called 'Crap In My Mouth, I Love It.'"

"Okay," says the bartender. "You can have the job, just as long as you don't tell anyone the names of the songs."

So the guy begins working nights at the bar, playing to full houses every night, and, true to his word, never revealing the titles of the songs. One night, though, he takes a break to go to the bathroom and forgets to zip up his pants afterwards, and his schlong is hanging out. A patron notices and approaches him.

"Do you know your pants are unzipped and your thing is hanging out?"

"Know it, pal?" says the piano player. "I wrote it!"

* * * *

A man scanned the crowd at a bar and spotted an attractive woman standing alone. He approached her and asked her name. "My name is Carmen," she told him.

"That's a beautiful name," he said. "Is it a family name?"

"No," she replied. "I gave it to myself. It reflects the things I like most - cars and men."

"What's your name?" she asked.

"Beerfuck," he said.

* * * *

Two women friends had gone out for a "girls' night out" and had been decidedly overenthusiastic on the cocktails. Incredibly drunk and walking home, they suddenly realized they both needed to pee. They were very near a graveyard and one of them suggested they do their business behind a headstone or something.

The first woman had nothing to wipe with so she took off her panties, used them and threw them away. Her friend was wearing an expensive underwear set and didn't want to ruin hers, but was lucky enough to salvage a large ribbon from a wreath that was on a grave and proceeded to wipe herself with it. After finishing, they made their way home.

The next day the first woman's husband phones the other husband and said, "These damn girls nights out have got to stop. My wife came home last night without her panties."

"That's nothing," said the other. "Mine came back with a greeting card stuck between the cheeks of her butt that said, *From all of us at the Fire Station, Well never forget you!*"

* * * *

A baby seal walks into a bar and sits down. "What can I get you?" asked the bartender.

"Anything but a Canadian Club," replied the seal.

* * * *

A guy walks into a bar where there is loud music playing. He spots a pretty girl at the end of the bar and approaches her. He says, "Would you like to dance?"

She replies, "I really don't like this song. And even if I did, I wouldn't dance with you."

To which the guy replies "I don't think you heard me correctly. I said you look fat in those pants."

* * * *

An obviously intoxicated gentleman staggers into a tavern and seats himself at the bar. After being served, he notices a woman sitting a few stools down. He motions the bartender over and says "Bartender, I'd like to buy that old douche bag down there a drink."

Somewhat offended, the bartender replies "Sir, I run a respectable establishment, and I don't appreciate you calling my female customers douche bags."

The man looked ashamed of himself and muttered "You're right, that was uncalled for . . . please allow me to buy the woman a cocktail."

"That's better" said the bartender and he approached the woman. "Ma'am, the gentleman down the bar would like to buy you a drink... what would you like?"

"How nice!" replied the woman, "I'll have a vinegar and water."

* * * *

At 3 a.m., a desk clerk at a hotel gets a call from a drunk guy asking what time the bar opens. "It opens at noon," answers the clerk. About an hour later he gets a call from the same guy, sounding even drunker.

"What time does the bar open?" he asks.

"Same time as before . . . noon." replies the clerk.

Another hour passes and he calls again, plastered "When joo shay the bar opins at?"

The clerk then answers, "It opens at noon, but if you can't wait, I can have room service send something up to you."

"No . . . I don't wanna git in . . . Ah wanna git OUT!!!"

* * * *

A man stomps into a bar, obviously angry. He growls at the bartender, "Gimme a beer," takes a slug, and shouts out, "All lawyers are assholes!"

A guy at the other end of the bar retorts, "You take that back!"

The angry man snarls, "Why? Are you a lawyer?"

The guy replies, "No, I'm an asshole!"

* * * *

A drunk staggers into a bar and says to the bartender, "I'd like to buy everyone in the bar a drink and get one for yourself too!"

The bartender makes the drinks and everyone raises their glass and yells "Cheers!" and downs their drinks.

The bartender says "That'll be $37.50."

The drunk says, "I don't have any money!"

This infuriates the bartender who then jumps over the bar and beats the living daylights out of the drunk and throws him out into the street.

The next day, the same drunk walks into the same bar and says, "I'd like to buy the whole bar a drink, and get one for yourself, too."

The bartender figures that maybe he was a little hard on the guy the day before and decides to give the guy the benefit of the doubt. He makes the drinks, and they all say, "Salute!" and down the drinks.

The bartender says, "That'll be $42.50."

The drunk replies by putting his thumb to his nose, wiggling his fingers, and making a loud raspberry noise followed by, "I don't have any money!"

This angers the bartender even more than the first time. He jumps over the bar and beats the hell out of the drunk and throws him out into the street onto his face, and kicks him a few times for good measure.

The next day the same drunk walks into the same bar, but before he can say anything the bartender says, "Let me guess, you want to buy the whole bar a drink and I should get one for myself, too, right?"

The drunk replies, "No way, you get too violent when you drink!"

* * * *

A Black, a Rabbi, a Pollock, a blonde, a Russian, a priest, and a nun walk into a bar.

The bartender says "What is this? Some kind of joke?"

* * * *

A guy walks into a bar with a pet alligator by his side. He puts the alligator up on the bar. He turns to the astonished patrons. "I'll make you a deal. I'll open this alligator's mouth and place my genitals inside. Then the gator will close his mouth for one minute. He'll then open his mouth and I'll remove my unit unscathed. In return for witnessing this spectacle, each of you will buy me a drink."

The crowd murmured their approval. The man stood up on the bar, dropped his trousers, and placed his privates in the alligator's open mouth. The gator closed his mouth as the crowd gasped. After a minute, the man grabbed a beer bottle and rapped the alligator hard on the top of its head. The gator opened his mouth and the man removed his genitals unscathed as promised. The crowd cheered, and the first of his free drinks were delivered. The man stood up again and made another offer. "I'll pay anyone $100 who's willing to give it a try".

A hush fell over the crowd. After a while, a hand went up in the back of the bar. A woman timidly spoke up, "I'll try, but you have to promise not to hit me on the head with the beer bottle."

* * * *

A woman walks in to a bar with a duck under her arm. The bartender says "Hey, you can't bring that dog in here."

The woman says, "This isn't a dog, it's a duck."

Bartender says, "I wasn't talking to you!"

* * * *

A man walks into a bar and asks the bartender, "If I show you a really good trick, will you give me a free drink?" The bartender considers it, then agrees. The man reaches into his pocket and pulls out a tiny rat. He reaches into his other pocket and pulls out a tiny piano. The rat stretches, cracks his knuckles, and proceeds to play the blues.

After the man finished his drink, he asked the bartender, "If I show you an even better trick, will you give me free drinks for the rest of the evening?" The bartender agrees, thinking that no trick could possibly be better than the first.

The man reaches into his pocket and pulls out a tiny rat. He reaches into his other pocket and pulls out a tiny piano. The rat stretches, cracks his knuckles, and proceeds to play the blues. The man reaches into another pocket and pulls out a small bullfrog, who begins to sing along with the rat's music.

While the man is enjoying his beverages, a stranger confronts him and offers him $100,000 for the bullfrog.

"Sorry," the man replies, "he's not for sale." The stranger increases the offer to $250,000 cash up front.

"No," he insists, "he's not for sale." The stranger again increases the offer, this time to $500,000 cash. The man finally agrees, and turns the frog over to the stranger in exchange for the money.

"Are you insane?" the bartender demanded. "That frog could have been worth millions to you, and you let him go for a mere $500,000!"

"Don't worry about it." the man answered. "The frog was really nothing special. You see, the rat's a ventriloquist."

* * * *

A big ol' Texas A&M cowboy is in a bar in Texas. He gets up to use the restroom. Once inside, he finds a Leprechaun. He grabs him up and says, "I got me a leprechaun! I get three wishes!"

The leprechaun replies, "Well, this is 2006. You get 3 wishes, and I get one from you." The cowboy agrees.

"What's your first wish?" says the leprechaun.

"I want all the cattle in Texas," says the cowboy.

"Okay what's your second wish?"

"I want all the land in Texas."

"Ummm, all right. you got it. Whats your third wish?"

"I want all the money in Texas."

"Well, okay, it's all yours. The land, money, and cattle. Now, for my wish," says the leprechaun.

"All right, what do you want?" says the cowboy.

The leprechaun says, "I want to fuck you in the ass."

The cowboy thinks about it and decides its worth it. He checks the stalls and closes the door. He goes into the stall bends over and faces the door. The leprechaun climbs up on the toilet and starts fucking him deep and hard. The leprechaun starts making small talk.

"Are ya married?" asks the leprechaun.

"Aaaahhhhh! Yep," says the cowboy through his obvious pain.

"Got kids?" asked the leprechaun.

"Uuuurrggghhhh! Yeah, two," says the cowboy.

"How old are ya?" asks the leprechaun.

"Eeeerrrrrrr! Ugh. Thirty-three," says the cowboy.

"Really? A little old to be believin' in leprechauns, ain't ya?"

* * * *

A new guy in town walks into a bar and reads a sign that hangs over the bar: *Free Beer For The Person Who Can Pass The Test!* So the guy asks the bartender what the test is.

Bartender says, "Well, first, you have to drink that whole gallon of pepper tequila, the whole thing at once and you can't make a face while doing it. Second, there's a 'gator out back with a sore tooth. You have to remove it with your bare hands. Third, there's a woman upstairs who's never had an orgasm. You gotta make things right for her."

The man says, "Well, as much as I would love free beer, I won't do it. You have to be nuts to drink a gallon of pepper tequila and the requirements get crazier from there."

Well, as time goes on and the man drinks a few, he asks, "Wherez zat teeqeelah?"

He grabs the gallon of tequilla with both hands, and downs it with a big slurp and tears streaming down his face.

Next, he staggers out back and soon all the people inside hear the most frightening roaring and thumping, then silence.

The man staggers back into the bar, his shirt ripped and big scratches all over his body. "Now," he says. "Where's that woman with the sore tooth?"

* * * *

A kilted Scotsman was walking down a country path after finishing off a considerable amount of alcohol at a local pub. As he staggered down the road, he felt quite sleepy and decided to take a nap with his back against a tree.

As he slept, two young lasses walking down the road heard the Scotsman snoring loudly. They saw him and one said, "I've always wondered what a Scotsman wears under his kilt."

She boldly walked over to the sleeping man, raised his kilt, and saw what nature had provided him at his birth. Her friend said, "Well, he has solved a great mystery for us, now! He must be rewarded!" So, she took a blue ribbon from her hair, and gently tied it around what nature had provided the Scotsman, and the two walked away.

Several minutes later, the Scotsman was awakened by the call of nature and walked around to the other side of the tree to relieve himself. He raised his kilt and saw where the blue ribbon was tied.

After several moments of bewilderment, the Scotsman said, "I dinna know where ya been laddie . . . but it's nice ta know ya won first prize!"

* * * *

Brenda O'Malley is home making dinner, as usual, when Tim Finnegan arrives at her door.

"Brenda, may I come in?" he asks. "I've somethin' to tell ya".

"Of course you can come in. You're always welcome, Tim. But where's my husband?"

"That's what I'm here to be telling ya, Brenda. There was an accident down at the Guinness brewery."

"Oh, God no!" cries Brenda. "Please don't tell me."

"I must, Brenda. Your husband Shamus is dead and gone. I'm sorry."

Finally, she looked up at Tim. "How did it happen, Tim?"

"It was terrible, Brenda. He fell into a vat of Guinness Stout and drowned."

"Oh my dear Jesus! But you must tell me true, Tim. Did he at least go quickly?"

"Well, Brenda . . . no. In fact, he got out three times to pee."

****

A man walks into a bar and sits down for a drink. The woman sitting next to him couldn't help but notice the sad look on his face as he orders a drink. She proceeds to ask him, "What's wrong?"

"My wife left me," the man replies.

"Oh, that is so sad, I am sorry to here that," says the woman. "Why did she leave you?"

"Well, to be honest, she said that I was too kinky."

The woman then says, "Well, you won't believe this, but just last year my husband left me, for the very same reason. What do you say we finish these drinks, head back to my place, and see what happens?"

The man agrees, And when they get back to her place, she tells him to make himself comfortable and proceeds to the bedroom. She decides to make the best of it, and pulls out her finest kinky outfit. Black leather boots that go to her knees. Crotchless panties, and a bustier in black patent leather. A spiked collar and long black gloves. She ties her hair back in a tight pony tail, grabs her whip and heads for the door.

As she walks out she sees the man just opening the door to leave. "Where are you going?" she asks. "I thought we were going to have some fun."

The man replies, "I already fucked your dog and shit in your purse. I'm out of here."

* * * *

The symphony orchestra was performing Beethoven's Ninth. In the piece, there's a long passage, about 20 minutes, during which the bass violinists have nothing to do.

Rather than sit around that whole time looking stupid, some bassists decided to sneak offstage and go to the tavern next door for a quick one. After slamming several beers in quick succession, one of them looked at his watch and said, "Hey! We need to get back!"

"No need to panic," said a fellow bassist. "I thought we might need some extra time, so I tied the last few pages of the conductor's score together with string. It will take him a few minutes to get it untangled."

A few moments later they staggered back to the concert hall and took their places in the orchestra. About this time, a member of the audience noticed the conductor seemed a bit edgy and said as much to her companion.

"Well, of course," said her companion. "Don't you see? It's the bottom of the Ninth, the score is tied, and the bassists are loaded."

JOKE ANALYSIS
BY DR. BROWN

Virtually every campus has a pub. Within the hallowed walls of this traditional drinking hole, events occur that are every bit as educational as those within the classrooms. I can still recall making the valuable discovery that kissing a girl with boilermaker vomit on her breath was, all things considered, better than not kissing a girl at all. Apparently she felt the same way as she quickly turned her attention to her also recently-purged girlfriend. As I stood watching the action and pulling a drink napkin across my tongue, Joe, a student so resistant to education that he actually serves as proof of its fallibility, shared this biscuit:

A Jew and a Chinaman are drinking at a bar, when all of a sudden the Jew hauls off and slugs the Chinaman in the face.

The Chinaman rubs his jaw and says, "What the hell was that for?"

"Pearl Harbor," replies the Jew.

"Pearl Harbor?" yells the Chinaman. "The Japanese bombed Pearl Harbor, you idiot! Not the Chinese!"

"Japanese. Chinese. What's the difference? You all look the same to me."

The two men continue drinking in silence for a while, when out of nowhere, the Chinaman hauls of and slugs the Jew in the face.

"What the hell was that for?" screams the Jew.

"The *Titanic*," replies the Chinaman.

"The *Titanic*? How in hell could I be responsible for that? The *Titanic* sunk when it hit a fucking iceberg!"

"Iceberg. Goldberg. What's the difference?"

It pains me to even comment on such a joke.

For what kind of shocking gaps in our education system exist that a man like Joe could believe that a Jewish man might actually resort to physical violence to right a perceived wrong, instead of relying on a treacherously potent combination of judicial action and constant whining?

Even more disturbingly, how could Joe possibly believe that any Western man could land a punch on a Chinaman? The Chinee, trained as they are from birth in the ways of either Shaolin or Wudan Kung Fu, are virtually immune to fisticuffs, especially from untrained combatants. Not a day goes by that a Chinaman isn't seeking revenge against his Master's assassin, or flying through bamboo trees chasing the elusive Jade Fox. And certainly in a bar, a Chinese Drunken Master is well-nigh invulnerable.

To be sure, there are instances of Hebrew Pugilists who might land a chance blow. One-time heavyweight champion of the world Mendoza the Jew springs to mind. And Geraldo Rivera's ability to break chairs with his nose is well-documented. But these are rare occasions indeed, comparable to such statistically insignificant occurrences as Meteoric Extinction Events and Welshmen Who Don't Fuck Sheep.

Moreover, even if the Chinaman were to somehow get caught flush on the face, he would never seek to redress the wrong immediately.

No, no! To the cultures of the Far East, revenge is a dish best served cold, and usually with broccoli.

Remember, patience and cruelty are the two unwavering hallmarks of the Orient, whose venerable and awful civilizations stretch back through the millennia, each dynasty founded upon the rock of fear. It is a certainty that, once smitten, the aggrieved Chinee would take his place back at the bar, smiling and inscrutable. He would bide his time for years until one day, far in the future, he'd seize his victim and subject him to tortures no Western mind could fathom. Perhaps our unfortunate Jewish tippler could expect the Death of 1000 Cuts. Or the infamous Water Torture. Or being forced to watch "the Joy Luck Club."

MEDI 370
CULTURE, HEALTH,
AND ILLNESS

Course:	MEDI 370 Culture, Health, and Illness
Semester:	Spring of every year
Credits:	3
Description:	Cross-cultural perspectives on the definition and treatment of illness. Course follows training from playing doctor to paying doctor. Patient treatment, healing environments and creating intimidating noises during the pulling on of rubber gloves are explored.
Dates:	FALL and SPRING - Open

We have all heard the phrase, "As long as you have your health." I'm not knocking health, but there are plenty "as you long as you haves" that are right up there. Your dick, for instance. You've got a choice, a wheelchair for life and a working dick or speed, agility and tiny urethra hole hidden above your testicles. What's it gonna be, friend, what's it gonna be? I, for one, would roll my bulk to bed and become the master of the lame-ass fuck.

—Steve

A man was visiting his wife in hospital where she has been in a coma for several years. On this visit, he decides to rub her left breast instead of just talking to her. When he does, she lets out a sigh.

The man runs out and tells the doctor who says this is a good sign and suggests he should try rubbing her right breast to see if there is any reaction. The man goes in and rubs her right breast and this brings a moan.

From this, the doctor suggests that the man should go in and try oral sex, saying he will wait outside as it is a personal act, and he doesn't want the man to be embarrassed.

The man goes in then comes out about five minutes later, white as a sheet and tells the doctor his wife is dead. The doctor asks what happened. The man replies, "She choked."

* * * *

A Fightin' Irish linebacker who has had a terrible football accident walks into a doctor's office. He has lost his penis, but the rest of the package is intact. He has met a girl who he feels is very special, but his shortcoming leads him to lack confidence.

"Doc, there's got to be something you can do for me?"

"Well, give me a week to do some research," says the doctor.

A week later, the man eagerly returns.

"Well, I'm afraid none of my colleagues could help you but I've got a friend who is a taxidermist," the doctor says. "He gave me the last 6-inches of an elephant trunk. It's your only option."

The linebacker has the operation and leaves the hospital to test out his new equipment. He takes his lady friend to a really nice restaurant. The couple is engaged in some light conversation and the man starts to feel pretty good about the situation.

They are looking at the wine list and the waiter brings them a basket of rolls. All of a sudden something comes out from under the table, grabs a roll, and disappears back under the table. The woman pushes her chair back and starts freaking out. To calm her, the linebacker says; "Don't be alarmed. It's a little trick, and I'm the only one who knows how to do it."

"That was pretty neat. Can you do it again?"

"I think so, but I don't know if my asshole can take another roll."

* * * *

An old lady came into her doctor's office and confessed to an embarrassing problem. "I fart all the time, Dr Johnson, but they're silent, and they have no odor. In fact, I've farted no less than six times since I've been here. What can I do?"

"Here's a prescription, Mrs. Barker. Take these pills three times a day for seven days. Then come back and see me in a week."

The next week, an upset Mrs. Barker marched into Dr Johnson's office, "Doctor, I don't know what was in those pills, but the problem is now much worse. I'm farting just as much and they're still silent, but now they smell terrible! What do you have to say for yourself?"

"Calm down, Mrs. Barker," replied the doctor soothingly. "Now that we've fixed your sinuses, we can begin to work on your hearing!"

* * * *

Mr. Smith goes to the doctor's office for his wife's test results. The lab tech told him, "I'm sorry sir, but there has been a mix-up. When we sent the sample from your wife to the lab, a sample from another Mrs. Smith was also sent, and now we're uncertain which one is your wife's. Frankly, the news is either bad or terrible."

"What do you mean?" asked the concerned spouse.

"Well," the medic explained, "one Mrs. Smith tested positive for Alzheimer's disease and the other for AIDS."

"Can we do the test over?" the husband cried.

"Normally, but your HMO won't pay for these expensive tests more than once," said the technician.

"Well, what am I supposed to do now?" Mr. Smith demanded.

The lab tech replied, "The HMO recommends that you drop your wife off in the middle of the woods. If she finds her way home, don't fuck her."

* * * *

A young woman in the maternity ward just prior to labor is asked by the midwife if she would like her husband to be present at the birth. "I'm afraid I don't have a husband," she replies.

"Okay. Do you have a boyfriend?" asks the midwife.

"No, no boyfriend either."

"Do you have a partner then?"

"No, I'm not attached; I'll be having my baby on my own." After the birth, the midwife again speaks to the young woman,

"You have a healthy bouncing baby girl, but I must warn you before you see her that the baby is black."

"Well," replies the girl, "I was very down on my luck, with no money and nowhere to live, and so I accepted a job in a porn film. The lead man was black."

"Oh, I'm very sorry, " says the midwife, "that's really none of my business, and I'm sorry that I have to ask you these awkward questions, but I must also tell you that the baby has blonde hair."

"Well, yes," the girl again replies, "you see the co-star in the movie was this Swedish guy."

"Oh, I'm sorry," the midwife repeats, "that's really none of my business either and I hate to pry further, but your baby also has slanted eyes."

"Yes," continues the girl, "there was a little Chinese man also in the movie, I really had no choice."

At this, the midwife again apologizes, collects the baby and presents her to the girl, who immediately proceeds to give the baby a slap on the butt. The baby starts crying, and the mother exclaims, "Thank God for that!"

"What do you mean?" says the midwife, shocked.

"Well, " says the girl extremely relieved, "I was afraid she was going to bark."

* * * *

A total babe goes to the gynecologist. The doctor takes one look at the woman and all of his professionalism goes out the window. He immediately asks her to undress. After she has disrobed, the doctor begins stroking her thigh. "Do you know what I'm doing?" he asks.

"Yes," she replies. "You're checking for any abrasions or abnormalities."

"That's right," says the doctor. Emboldened, he then begins to fondle her breasts. "Do you know what I'm doing now?"

"You're checking for any lumps or breast cancer," she replies.

"Correct," says the doctor.

Deciding to go for broke, he mounts her and begins having sex with her. "Do you know what I'm doing now?"

"Yes," she says. "You're getting herpes—which is what I came here about in the first place."

* * * *

A woman accompanied her husband to the doctor's office. After the checkup, the doctor took the wife aside and said, "Your husband is suffering from severe, long-term stress and it's affecting his cardiovascular system. He's a good candidate for either a heart attack or a stroke. If you don't do the following four things, your husband will surely die. First, each morning, fix him a healthy breakfast and send him off to work in a good mood. Second, at lunch time, make him a warm, nutritious meal and put him in a good frame of mind before he goes back to work. Third, for dinner, fix an especially nice meal, and don't burden him with household chores. Fourth, and most important for invigorating him and relieving stress, have sex with him several times a week and satisfy his every whim in bed."

On the way home in the car, the husband turned to his wife and asked, "So, I saw the doctor talking to you, and he sure seemed serious. What did he tell you?"

"You're going to die," she replied.

* * * *

A male patient is lying in bed in the hospital, wearing an oxygen mask over his mouth and nose, still heavily sedated from a difficult, four hour surgical procedure. A young, student nurse appears to give him a partial sponge bath. "Nurse," he mumbles, from behind the mask. "Are my testicles black?"

Embarrassed, the young nurse replies, "I don't know, sir. I'm only here to wash your upper body and feet."

He struggles to ask again, "Nurse, are my testicles black?" Concerned that he may elevate his vitals from worry about his testicles, she overcomes her embarrassment and sheepishly pulls back the covers.

She raises his gown, holds his penis in one hand and his testicles in the other, lifting and moving them around. Then, she takes a close look and says, "There's nothing wrong with them, sir!"

The man pulls off his oxygen mask, smiles at her and says very slowly, "Thank you very much. That was wonderful, but, listen very, very closely. A r e - m y - t e s t - r e s u l t s - b a c k?"

* * * *

A gynecologist was getting sick of his job and decided that he needed a career change. He'd always enjoyed tinkering with engines so he thought he'd become a mechanic. So he went along to mechanics school, and the final test was to strip the engine completely and reassemble it back into perfect working order. So our gynecologist friend did the test and anxiously awaited his results. The day he received the results, he got quite a surprise — he got 150%. He quickly phoned the instructor and asked about the high mark. The instructor said, "No, that's right. First, I gave you 50% for stripping down the engine — a very thorough job. Next, I gave you 50% for reassembling it — a fantastic job really. And then I gave you a 50% bonus for doing it all through the tail pipe."

* * * *

When my girlfriend was rushed to the hospital unexpectedly, she asked me to bring her a few items from home. One item on her list was "comfortable underwear."

Not sure what she considered comfortable, I asked, "How will I know which ones to pick?"

"Hold them up and imagine them on me, " she answered. "If you smile, put them back."

* * * *

Once there was a midget who complained to his buddy that his testicles ached all the time. As he was always talking about his aching testicles, his friend suggested that he go to the doctor and see what he could do to relieve the problem. The midget took his advice, went to the doctor and told him what the problem was. The doctor told him to drop his pants and he would have a look.

The midget dropped his pants. The doctor put him up onto the examining table and proceeded to look for the trouble. The doc put one finger under his left testicle and told the midget to cough, which he did.

"Ah! Ah!" mumbled the doc and putting his finger under the right one asked him to cough again, which he did.

"Ah! Ah!" said the doctor and reached for his surgical scissors.

Snip, snip, snip on the right side.

Snip, snip, snip on the left side.

He told the midget to pull up his pants and see if it still ached. The midget was delighted as he walked around the doc's office and his testicles were not aching. "What did you do Doc?" he asked.

The doc replied, "I cut two inches off the top of your cowboy boots."

* * * *

After a few years of married life, a man finds that he is unable to perform for his wife. He goes to his doctor, and his doctor tries a few medications, but nothing works. Finally the doctor says to him, "This is all in your mind," and refers him to a psychiatrist.

After a few visits with the psychiatrist, the psychiatrist confesses he can not figure out what is wrong. The psychiatrist decides to refer him to a witch doctor.

The witch doctor says, "I can cure this!" He throws some powder on a flame, and there is a flash with billowing blue smoke. The witch doctor says, "This is powerful healing, but you can only use it once a year. All you have to do is say '123,' and it will rise for as long as you wish."

The guy then asks the witch doctor, "What happens when it's over?"

The witch doctor says, "All you or your partner has to say is '1234,' and it will go down. But be warned it will not work again for a full year." The guy goes home and that night he is ready to surprise his wife with the good news. So, as he is lying in bed with his wife, he says, "123." Suddenly his penis gets a huge erection. With that, his wife turns over and says, "What did you say '123' for?"

* * * *

A woman and a baby were in the doctor's examining room, waiting for the doctor to come in for the baby's first exam. The doctor arrived, examined the baby, checked his weight, and being a little concerned, asked if the baby was breast-fed or bottle-fed.

"Breast-fed," she replied.

"Well, strip to your waist," the doctor ordered. She did. He pinched her nipples, then pressed, kneaded, and rubbed both breasts for a while in a detailed examination.

Motioning to her to get dressed, he said, "No wonder this baby is underweight. You don't have any milk."

"I know," she said, "I'm his Grandma, but I'm glad I came."

* * * *

The doctor took Dan into the room and said, "Dan, I have some good news and some bad news."

"Oh, no. Give me the good news, I guess," Dan replied.

"They're going to name a disease after you."

* * * *

A woman is in the delivery room in labor. One final push and the baby comes out. Above the baby's pitiful first cries, she hears the horrified gasps of the doctor and shrieks of the nurses. The baby is rushed away before she can see it.

Later, a doctor comes in and says, "I'm afraid there's a . . . problem with your new son. It seems he was born without a body."

She stammers, "You mean . . ."

"Yes," the doctor says, "he has no body. He's just a head. But, on the bright side, he's a perfectly healthy and normal head."

The years pass by, and the mother takes to putting her son (now a teenaged head) on a table upstairs near the window so he can look out at the other children playing.

One day, the phone rings. It's the hospital. A surgeon informs the woman that there has been a horrible accident, and a young man has been completely decapitated. There is a good chance that her son's head can be attached to the victim's body! She drops the phone, runs upstairs to where her son has rested most of his life and says, "Son! I have the most wonderful surprise for you!"

The kid looks up at her and replies, "I hope it's not another hat."

* * * *

Jim and Edna were both patients in a mental hospital. One day while they were walking past the hospital swimming pool, Jim suddenly jumped into the deep end. He sank to the bottom of the pool and stayed there. Edna promptly jumped in to save him. She swam to the bottom and pulled Jim out.

When the hospital director became aware of Edna's heroic act, she immediately ordered that Edna be discharged from the hospital because she now considered Edna to be mentally stable.

A few days later, the director went to visit the now-free Edna with some bad news.

She tells her, "Edna, I'm sorry but Jim, the patient you saved, hung himself in the bathroom with his bathrobe belt right after you saved him. I am sorry, but he's dead."

Edna replied, "Oh relax, silly. He didn't hang himself. I put him there to dry."

* * * *

A woman enrolled in nursing school is attending an anatomy class. The subject of the day is involuntary muscles. The instructor, hoping to perk up the students a bit, asks her if she knows what her asshole does when she's having an orgasm.

"Sure," she says, "He's at home taking care of the kids."

* * * *

Doctor Dave slept with one of his patients and felt guilty all day long. No matter how much he tried to forget about it, he couldn't. The guilt and sense of betrayal was overwhelming. But every once in a while he'd hear an internal, reassuring voice that said, "Dave, don't worry about it. You aren't the first doctor to sleep with one of their patients and you won't be the last. And you're single. Let it go . . ."

But invariably the other voice would bring him back to reality. "Dave, you're a vet."

* * * *

A nurse walks into a bank, preparing to sign a check. She reaches in her pocket and pulls out a rectal thermometer and says, "Well that's great. Some asshole's got my pen."

* * * *

Doctor: Nurse, how is that little boy doing, the one who swallowed ten quarters?
Nurse: No change yet.

* * * *

One morning, the renowned psychiatrist was holding a group consultation with three young mothers and their small children. "All three of you have obsessions," he proceeded to tell them.

To the first mother, the shrink said, "Your obsession is eating. Why you've even named your daughter Candy."

The second woman, the shrink claimed, was obsessed by money. "Again, it manifests itself in your child's name, Penny."

At this point, the third mother arose and, taking her little boy by the hand, whispered, "Let's go, Dick."

* * * *

A man hasn't been feeling well, so he goes to his doctor for a complete checkup. Afterward, the doctor comes out with the results.

"I'm afraid I have some very bad news," the doctor says. "You're dying, and you don't have much time left."

"Oh, that's terrible!" says the man. "How long have I got?"

"Ten," the doctor says sadly.

"Ten?" the man asks. "Ten what? Months? Weeks? What?!"

"Nine . . ."

* * * *

A middle school science teacher, Mrs. Parks, asked her class, "Which human body part increases to 10 times its size when stimulated?"

Little Mary stood up, angry, and said, "You should not be asking 6th graders a question like that! I'm going to tell my parents, and they will go and tell the principal, and you'll get fired!"She then sat back down.

Mrs. Parks ignored her, and asked the question again, "Which body part increases to 10 times its size when stimulated?"

Little Mary's mouth fell open, and she said to those around her, "Boy, is she gonna get in big trouble!"

The teacher continued to ignore her and said to the class "Anybody?"

Finally, Billy stood up, looked around nervously, and said, "The body part that increases to 10 times its size when stimulated is the pupil of the eye."

Mrs. Parks said, "Very good, Billy."

Then she turned to Mary and continued, "As for you, young lady, I have three things to say: First, you have a dirty mind. Second, you didn't read your homework. And third, one day you are going to be VERY, VERY disappointed."

* * * *

As the manager of our hospital's softball team, I was responsible for returning equipment to the proper owners at the end of the season. When I walked into the surgery department carrying a bat that belonged to one of the surgeons, I passed several patients and their families in a waiting area. Unable to resist, I walked up to a patient giving his doctor a hard time before surgery and said, "Hi, I'm your anesthesiologist."

* * * *

Two parents, both doctors, take their son on a vacation to a nude beach so he can become comfortable with the human body. The father goes for a walk on the beach and the son goes and plays in the water. The son comes running up to his mom and says, "Mommy, I saw ladies with boobies a lot bigger than yours!"

The mom smiles and says, "The bigger they are, the dumber they are." So he goes back to play.

Minutes later he runs back and says, "Mommy, I saw men with dingers a lot bigger than Daddy's!"

The mom says, "The bigger they are, the dumber they are." So he goes back to play.

Several minutes later he comes running back and says, "Mommy, I just saw Daddy talking to the dumbest lady I ever saw and the more and more he talked, the dumber he got!"

* * * *

A father asks his 10-year-old son if he knows the truth about the birds and the bees. "I don't want to know!" the child says, bursting into tears. "Promise me you won't tell me!"

Confused, the father asks what's wrong. "Oh, dad," the boy sobs. "When I was six, I got the 'There's no Santa' speech. At seven, I got the 'There's no Easter Bunny' speech. When I was eight, you hit me with the 'There's no tooth fairy' speech. If you're going to tell me that adults don't really fuck, I'll have nothing left to live for."

* * * *

A Marine, injured and hospitalized in Afghanistan recently received a "Dear John" letter from his girlfriend back home. It read as follows:

Dear Ricky,

I can no longer continue our relationship. The distance between us is just too great. I must admit that I have cheated on you twice since you've been gone, and it's not fair to either of us. I'm sorry. Please return the picture of me that I sent to you.

Love, Becky

The Marine, with hurt feelings, asked his fellow Marines for any snapshots they could spare of their girlfriends, sisters, ex-girlfriends, aunts, cousins, etc. In addition to the picture of Becky, Ricky included all the other pictures of the pretty gals he had collected from his buddies. There were 57 photos in that envelope along with this note:

Dear Becky,

I'm so sorry, but I can't quite remember who the fuck you are. Please take your picture from the pile, and send the rest back to me.

* * * *

Once upon a time, there was this sperm called Brian. Brian was a very health-conscious sperm who spent all his time doing push-ups, sit-ups, somersaults and generally charging around the testicle being fit, while all the other sperms just slobbed about the place doing nothing.

One day, one of the other sperms roused himself long enough to become curious, and asked Brian why he exercised all day. Brian said "Look pal, only one sperm gets to make a woman pregnant, and when the right time comes, I'm gonna be the one."

A few days later, they all felt themselves getting hotter and hotter and they knew that it was getting to be their time to go. Then they were abruptly released and sure enough, there was Brian swimming far ahead of all the others. All of a sudden Brian stopped, turned round and began to swim back with all his might. "Go back! Go back!" he screamed, "It's a blow job!"

* * * *

Q. What's green and eats nuts?
A. Syphilis

* * * *

Jim decided to propose to Sandy, but prior to her acceptance, Sandy had to confess to her man about her childhood illness. She informed Jim that she suffered a disease that left her breasts at maturity of a 12 year old. He stated that it was okay because he loved her so much.

However, Jim felt this was also the time for him to open up and admit that he also had a deformity. Jim looked Sandy in the eyes and said, "I too have a problem. My penis is the same size as an infant, and I hope you could deal with that once we are married."

She said, "Yes, I will marry you and learn to live with your infant-size penis."

Sandy and Jim got married and they could not wait for the honeymoon. Jim whisked Sandy off to their hotel suite and they started touching, teasing, holding one another...

As Sandy put her hands in Jim's pants, she began to scream and ran out of the room!

Jim ran after her to find out what was wrong. "You told me your penis was the size of an infant!" she said.

"Yes it is . . . 8 pounds, 7 ounces, 19 inches long!"

* * * *

A guy goes for his annual check-up, and about a week later his doctor calls him in to give him the results. "Well," says the doc, "You're in pretty good health. However I do have some good news and bad news for you."

"Give me the good news first," requests the guy.

"Your penis is three inches longer than it was on your last physical."

"That's great!" exclaims the guy, "But what's the bad news?"

The doctor replies, "It's malignant!"

* * * *

This woman goes into a funeral home to make arrangements for her husband's funeral. She tells the director that she wants her husband to be buried in a dark blue suit.

He asks, "Wouldn't it just be easier to bury him in the black suit that he's wearing?"

"No," she insists as she hands him a check to buy one. "It must be blue."

When she comes back for the wake, she sees her husband in the coffin and he is wearing a beautiful blue suit. She tells the director how much she loves the suit and asks how much it cost.

He says, "Actually, it didn't cost anything. The funniest thing happened. As soon as you left, another corpse was brought in, this one wearing a blue suit. I noticed that they were about the same size, and asked the other widow if she would mind if her husband were buried in a black suit. She said that was fine with her . . . so I switched the heads."

* * * *

"How come you're late?" asks the bartender as the blonde waitress walks in the door.

"It was awful," she explains. "I was walking down Elm Street and there was this terrible accident. A man was lying in the middle of the street. He'd been thrown from his car. His leg was broken, his skull was fractured, and there was blood everywhere. Thank God I took that first-aid course and all my training came back to me in a minute."

"What did you do?" asks the bartender.

"I sat down and put my head between my knees to keep from fainting!"

* * * *

Two gay men decide to have a baby. They mix their sperm, then have a surrogate mother artificially inseminated.

When the baby is born, they rush to the hospital. Two dozen babies are in the ward, 23 of which are crying and screaming. One, over in the corner, is smiling serenely.

A nurse comes by and, to the gays' delight, she points out the happy child as theirs.

"Isn't it wonderful?" Brad exclaims. "All these unhappy children, and ours is so happy."

The nurse says, "He's happy now. But just wait until we take the pacifier out of his ass."

* * * *

Q. What's a birth control pill?
A. The other thing a woman can put in her mouth to keep from getting pregnant.

* * * *

Two men are in court on drug charges. The judge says, "If, over the weekend, you can persuade enough people to give up drugs, I'll let you two off."

Back in court on Monday, the judge asks for their results.

"I persuaded ten people to give up drugs forever," the first man says.

"That's great," the judge replies. "What did you tell them?"

"I drew two circles . . . one big, one small. I told them the big circle was their brain before drugs, and the little circle was their brain after drugs."

The other defendant says, "I got one hundred people to give up drugs!"

"One hundred! How?" asks the judge.

"Well, I drew the same two circles. I pointed to the small circle and said, 'This is your asshole before prison . . .'"

JOKE ANALYSIS
BY DR. BROWN

No field of literary criticism has been untouched by the influence of Postmodern, structuralist theory, and joke analysis is no exception. A chicken crosses a road, to be sure, but what is the meaning of "the other side?" Perhaps it represents the chicken's latent homosexual urges - urges that it never had a chance to explore, since, being a chicken, it would have been rejected admission to every university it applied to, even state agricultural campuses.

Why such "crit" giants as Foucault continue to avoid applying critical theory to the canon of modern humor is hard to fathom. Foucault apologists, of whom there are legion, will probably rest their rebuttals on the fact that he has been dead for 29 years.

While involuntarily eavesdropping on the inter-urinal blather of two THC-saturated sophomores, I was gifted with a joke ("The Bedwetter and the Doctor"), which admirably illustrates the principle of how a joke must be considered in the totality of its environment:

This lady is having a bed-wetting problem, so she decides to go to the doctor. The doctor tells her to go and get undressed and wait for him in the other room. When the doctor goes into the room he tells the lady to stand on her head facing the mirror.

She figures he is a doctor and gets in front of the mirror. The doctor goes over to the lady and rests his chin between her legs and looks in the mirror. After a few minutes he pulls away and tells the lady to go ahead and put her clothes back on and he will talk to her when she is dressed.

The lady puts her clothes on and asks the doctor what is wrong with her.

He tells her that she needs to quit drinking before she goes to bed.

The lady asks the doctor why he had her get naked in front of the mirror and stand on her head.

He replies, "I wanted to see how I would look with a beard."

Perhaps in some societies, at some juncture in history, this joke could have been considered funny. But not in today's America.

Given the prevalence of stylized pubic haircuts, it is highly unlikely that our gynecologist could get any idea of how he would look with a normal beard. A brief survey of vaginal hair can easily be undertaken at any local gentlemen's club (conversely, such a survey is virtually impossible to arrange elsewhere). There for the price of a $20 entrance fee and two $8 sodas, the field scientist will quickly discover that half of today's women choose to groom their genitalia in what is commonly referred to as a "landing strip."

Thus, the odds are 50% that the good doctor will only be able to consider what his facial features would look like should he grow the facial hair equivalent: i.e. A "King Tut." This is an uncommon choice of facial foliage, propounded mostly by Yale Egyptologists who turn into super-villains when bonked on the head with a large vase, as well as musicians from Orange County.

As for the other half of today's women, my results indicate that they prefer to dance for money in a completely shorn state.

Thus, if the doctor's reply were "I'd like to see how I would look like if a snail attacked my chin," or "I always wondered what I'd look like if a camel kicked me," or "if I'd fallen face first into taco stand," or "if I applied a novelty axe wound to my lower mandible," then verisimilitude would be established. But the chance of the doctor seeing a useful beard sample is minimal, particularly given that the beard of choice for most men today is a goatee.

To be fair, if the woman in question is an older lady, she might still have the grooming habits of a bygone era - in other words, none at all. Alas, this too is problematic. For if one were to take recorded visual images of a woman's pubic hair from the 1970's (perhaps obtained from a movie such as *Behind the Green Door*), then extrapolate what such an area would look like after a further 30 years of unchecked growth, one comes away with a disturbing mental image indeed.

Unless the doctor were planning on becoming the fourth member of ZZ Top, or desired to spend his weekends engaging in Civil War reenactments, it is unlikely that he would risk losing his medical license by dipping his chin into a clam with a beard as long as Rebbe Schneerson.

ZOOL 511
ANIMAL SCIENCE
FOR VETERINARIANS

Course:	ZOOL 511 Animal Science for Veterinarians
Semester:	Fall of every year
Credits:	2
Restrictions:	Open only to graduate-professional students in the College of Veterinary Medicine and sadists.
Description:	Husbandry of domestic, laboratory, and zoo animals. Managerial systems in animal agriculture. Animal husbandry, wifendry and childandry. Mating habits, sedation and recreational euthanasia.
Dates:	FALL - Open

There is nothing more fun than the anthropomorphosis of animals. We pretend that ducks can talk, monkeys can bargain, and football players can pass math. Then of course, there's sex; interbreed, out of breed, with animals, with animals watching, with people dressed as animals . . . and that's just last night at my place!

— *Steve*

A young American Indian was wondering where he got his name. He went to his grandfather, the tribal chief, and posed that question to him. The old man said, "Do you see Running Deer over there playing by the stream? That was the first thing she saw when she came out of her mother's womb. And your friend Chasing Shadows? It was the sky dancing on the earth. Why do you ask, Two Dogs Fucking?"

* * * *

Three dogs are at the vet in the waiting room. When the first dog asks the second dog what he's in for, he answers, "My master bought a brand new carpet the other day, and at the first opportunity I soiled it, so now I've been brought here to be put to sleep. So what are you here for?"

The first dog replies grimly, "I'm also being put to sleep. My master had a table with a collection of expensive vases and while I was chasing my tail I accidentally bumped into the table and broke them all."

The two dogs then look over and ask the third dog what he's in for.

The third dog answers, "The reason I'm here is the other day my master stepped out of the shower and she bent over. I couldn't resist, so I jumped her from behind and took her like a wild animal!"

"So I guess you're also here to be put to sleep?" says the first dog.

The third dog answers, "Nope, I'm here to get my nails done."

* * * *

A Welsh man goes in the bedroom with a sheep under his arm and says, "See, dear? This is the pig I have to shag when you have a headache."

His wife returns, "I think you will find that's a sheep, dear."

He replies, "I think you will find I wasn't talking to you."

* * * *

Two fleas from Detroit had an agreement to meet every winter in Miami for a vacation. Last year, when one flea gets to Miami, he's all blue, shivering and shaking, damn near frozen to death! The other flea asks him, "What the hell happened to you?"

The first flea says, "I rode down here from Detroit in the mustache of a guy on a Harley."

The other flea responds saying, " That's the worst way to travel! Try what I do. Go to the Metro airport bar. Have a few drinks. While you're there, look for a nice stewardess. Crawl up her leg and nestle in where it's warm and cozy. You'll be in Miami in no time. It's the best way to travel that I can think of." The first flea thanks the second flea, and says he will give it a try next winter.

A year goes by . . . When the first flea shows up in Miami he is all blue and shivering and shaking again. Damn near frozen to death. The second flea says, "Didn't you try what I told you?"

"Yes," says the first flea, "I did exactly as you said. I went to the Metro airport bar. I had a few drinks. Finally, this nice young stewardess came in. I crawled right up to her warm cozy spot. It was so nice and warm that I fell asleep immediately. When I woke up, I was back in the mustache of the guy on the Harley."

* * * *

An ant is walking down the path through the jungle one day when he spies an elephant caught up in a hunter's trap. The elephant cries out, "Help! Help!"

The ant goes up to him and says, "I will help you but you have to let me do anything I want." So the elephant, figuring he has nothing to lose at this point, agrees.

The ant then chews through the trap and frees the now very grateful elephant. "Thank you so much, now what would you like to do?" says the elephant.

"I want to do you in the ass" says the ant.

The elephant looks at the tiny little ant and says "What the hell, how much could this hurt?" So the ant climbs up the elephant's back and goes about his business.

A monkey in a tree right overhead sees the whole thing and laughs so hard that a coconut falls down toward the elephant and hits him square in the head. The poor elephant cries out "OW!"

And the ant yells, "Take it all bitch!"

* * * *

A man was leaving a 7-11 with his morning coffee and newspaper when he noticed a most unusual funeral procession approaching the nearby cemetery. A long black hearse was followed by a second long black hearse about 50 feet behind. Behind the second hearse was a solitary man walking a pitbull on a leash. Behind him were 200 men walking single file. The guy couldn't stand the curiosity. He respectfully approached the man walking the dog and said, "Sir, I know now is a bad time to disturb you, but I've never seen a funeral like this. Whose funeral is it?"

The man replied, "Well, that first hearse is for my wife."

"What happened to her?"

The man replied, "My dog attacked and killed her."

He inquired further, "Well, who is in the second hearse?"

The man answered, "My mother-in-law. She was trying to help my wife when the dog turned on her."

A poignant and thoughtful moment of silence passes between the two men.

"Sir, could I borrow that dog?"

"Get in line."

* * * *

A rabbit one day managed to break free from the laboratory where he had been born and brought up. As he scurried away from the fencing of the compound, he felt grass under his little feet and saw the dawn breaking for the first time in his life. "Wow, this is great," he thought.

It wasn't long before he came to a hedge and, after squeezing under it he saw a wonderful sight: lots of other bunny rabbits, all free and nibbling at the lush grass.

"Hey," he called. "I'm a rabbit from the laboratory and I've just escaped. Are you wild rabbits?"

"Yes. Come and join us," they cried. Our friend hopped over to them and started eating the grass. It tasted so good.

"What else do you wild rabbits do?" he asked.

"Well," one of them said. "You see that field there? It's got carrots growing in it. We dig them up and eat them." This he couldn't resist and he spent the next hour eating the most succulent carrots. They were wonderful.

Later, he asked them again, "What else do you do?"

"You see that field there? It's got lettuce growing in it. We eat it as well." The lettuce tasted just as good, and he returned a while later completely full.

"Is there anything else you guys do?" he asked.

One of the other rabbits came a bit closer to him and spoke softly. "There's one other thing you must try. You see those rabbits there," he said, pointing to the far corner of the field. "They're girls. We shag them. Go and try it."

Well, our friend spent the rest of the morning screwing his little heart out until, completely knackered, he staggered back over to the guys. "That was fantastic," he panted.

"So are you going to live with us then?" one of them asked.

"I'm sorry, I had a great time but I can't." The wild rabbits all stared at him, a bit surprised.

"Why? We thought you liked it here."

"I do," our friend replied. "But I'm dying for a cigarette."

* * * *

A man wakes up one morning to find a gorilla on his roof. So he looks in the Yellow Pages and, sure enough, there's an ad for "Gorilla Removers." He calls the number, and the gorilla remover says he'll be over in thirty minutes.

The gorilla remover arrives, and gets out of his van. He's got a ladder, a baseball bat, a shotgun and a mean old pit bull. "What are you going to do?" the homeowner asks.

"I'm going to put this ladder up against the roof, then I'm going to go up there and knock the gorilla off the roof with this baseball bat. When the gorilla falls off, the pit bull is trained to grab his testicles and not let go. The gorilla will then be subdued enough for me to put him in the cage in the back of the van." So the guy puts the ladder up, gets the bat and the shotgun and walks towards the ladder. As he gets to the base of the ladder, he hands the shotgun to the homeowner.

"What's the shotgun for?" asks the homeowner.

"If the gorilla knocks me off the roof, shoot the dog!"

* * * *

Bob calls his buddy Sam, the horse rancher, and says he is sending a friend over to look at a horse.

Sam asks, "How will I recognize him?"

"That's easy. He's a midget with a speech impediment."

So, the midget shows up at the ranch, and Sam asks him if he's looking for a male or female horse.

"A female horth," So he shows him a prized filly. "Nith lookin horth, can I thee her eyeth?"

Sam picks up the midget, and he gives the horse's eyes the once over. "Nith eyeth, can I thee her earzth?"

So he picks the little fella up again, and shows him the horse's ears. "Nith earzth, can I see her mouf?"

The rancher is gettin' pretty ticked off by this point, but he wants to make the sale, so he picks him up again, and shows him the horse's mouth. "Nice mouf. Can I see her twat?" Totally mad at this point, Sam grabs the midget under his arms, and rams the midget's head as far in as he can up the horse's twat, pulls him out, and slams him on the ground!

The midget gets up, sputtering and coughing. "Perhapth I should rephrazthe that... Can I thee her wun awound a widdle bit?"

* * * *

After attending the funeral of a mouse killed while playing football, three mice, one from England, one from Scotland and one from Ireland, are sitting at a bar trying to impress each other with how tough they are.

The English mouse throws down a shot of bourbon, slams the empty glass onto the bar, turns to the Scottish mouse and says, "When I see a mousetrap, I lie on my back and set it off with my foot. When the bar comes down, I catch it in my teeth, bench press it twenty times to work up an appetite, and then make off with the cheese."

The Scottish mouse orders up two shots of tequila, drinks them down one after the other, slams both glasses onto the bar, turns to the English mouse and replies, "Oh yeah? When I see rat poison, I collect as much as I can, take it home, grind it up to a powder, and add it to my coffee each morning so I can get a good buzz going for the rest of the day."

The English mouse and the Scottish mouse then turn to the Irish mouse. The Irish mouse finishes the Guinness he has in front of him, lets out a long sigh and says to the two, "I don't have time for this bullshit, I'm going home to fuck the cat."

* * * *

A blonde was driving to the store when she saw a guy with two monkeys. She pulled over and asked if he needs help.

"Yes I do," he told her. "My car broke down and I need to get these monkeys to the zoo. If I give you $50, will you please take these monkeys to the zoo for me?"

"Sure," she replied. So she put the monkeys in her car and drove off. When the guy got his car fixed he started driving towards the zoo when he came across the same blonde walking down the streets holding the monkeys' hands.

"Hey I paid you $50 to take them to the zoo," he told her when he pulled up beside her.

"We did go to the zoo. But we had money left over so now we are going to the movies," she replied.

* * * *

A farmer is giving his wife last-minute instructions before heading to town to do chores. "That fellow from Sematol will be along this afternoon to inseminate one of the cows. I've hung a nail by the right stall so you'll know which one I want him to impregnate." Satisfied that even his mentally challenged wife could understand the instructions, the farmer left for town.

That afternoon, the 'inseminator' arrives, and the wife dutifully takes him out to the barn and directly to the stall with the nail. "This is the cow right here, " she tells him.

"What's the nail for?" the guy asks.

Replies the wife, "I guess its to hang up your pants."

* * * *

Late one night, a burglar broke into a house that he thought was empty. He tiptoed through the living room, then froze in his tracks when he heard a loud voice say, "Jesus is watching you."

Frantically, he looked around the house. Finally, in a dark corner, he spotted a parrot in a bird cage.

"Was that you who said Jesus is watching me?"

"Yes," replied the parrot.

The burglar breathed a sigh of relief, then asked, "What's your name?"

"Clarence," said the bird.

"That's a dumb name for a parrot," sneered the burglar.

"What idiot named you Clarence?"

"The same idiot who named the Doberman Jesus."

* * * *

A city slicker decided to give up the hustle and bustle of city life and become a pig farmer. He bought a dozen pigs, a farm, and a truck. He asked the local vet how he'd know when the pigs are pregnant. "When they're rolling around in the mud," replied the vet.

After a couple of weeks, there were no pigs rolling in the mud, so he goes to the vet again. The vet told him that if he screws the pigs, that will get them hot and bothered and soon he'll have pregnant sows all over the place. Not wanting anybody to see him, the guy loads all the pigs in the truck drives off to a secluded spot and fucks every one of the pigs.

A week later . . . no pigs rolling in the mud, so he takes the pigs to the secluded spot again and fucks all the pigs. Another week goes by and no pigs rolling in the mud. He once again takes the pigs to the secluded spot and fucks every pig TWICE this time. The next day, being very tired from his adventure, he asks his wife, "Honey, look out the window and tell me if there are any pigs rolling around in the mud?"

The wife replied, "Nope, but all the pigs are in the back of the truck and one of them is honking the horn!"

* * * *

One evening, a man walks into a bar with an octopus and lays down $500 and says, "My octopus can play any instrument you put in front of him."

Hearing this, a man walks up and puts a guitar in front of the octopus. Puzzled for a second the octopus grabs its and plays a riff like Jimi Hendrix would play.

Another guys walks up laughs and hands the octopus a trumpet. The octopus looks at it for a second and starts playing a song by Louis Armstrong.

Another guy hears about the bet at another bar across the street, runs out to his car and then to the bar where the octopus is. He then walks up to the bar, lays down his money, and hands the octopus a set of bag pipes. Very puzzled, the octopus sits back and just stares at the instrument. The owner expecting that he is about to lose his money, leans over to the octopus and says, "Hey, can you play this thing or not?"

Still looking puzzled the octopus looks at his owner and says, "Play it? If I can figure out how to get its pajamas off, I'm going to fuck it."

* * * *

A panda bear walks into a cafe and orders a sandwich and a drink. After he is finished eating, the waiter comes over to bring him the check. When the waiter arrives at the table, he just starts to ask, "Would you like any des..." when the panda bear reaches into his fur, pulls out a gun, and shoots the waiter dead.

The panda bear then wipes off his chin with his napkin, gets up, and starts to walk out. Just as he is about to go through the door, the manager grabs him. "Wait a minute!" he yells, "You just killed my best waiter! Besides that, you didn't even pay for your sandwich!"

The panda bear grasps the manager by the throat, jacks him up, and growls, "Hey, man! I'm a PANDA! Do you know what that means? Why don't you look it up!"

At this, the panda walks out the door and ambles down the street.

The manager, shaken, returns to his office and consults a dictionary. He reads:

"Panda - a large mammal of the Asian mountain forests related to raccoons and true bears and characterized by bold black and white markings. Eats shoots and leaves."

* * * *

A man and a woman were driving down the road arguing about his deplorable infidelity when suddenly the woman reaches over and slices the man's penis off and angrily tosses it out the car window.

Driving behind the couple is a man and his 12-year-old daughter. The little girl is just chatting away at her father when all of a sudden, the penis smacks against the windshield, sticks for a moment, then flies off.

Surprised, the daughter asks her father, "Daddy, what was that?"

Not wanting to expose his twelve-year-old daughter to anything sexual at such a young age, the father replies, "It was only a bug, honey."

The daughter sits with a confused look on her face and, after a few minutes says, "Sure had a big dick, didn't it?"

* * * *

Mary received a parrot as a gift. The parrot was fully-grown with a very bad attitude and worse vocabulary. Every other word was a curse: those that weren't curses were to say the least, rude.

Mary tried to change the bird's attitude by constantly saying polite things and playing soft music . . . anything she could think of. Nothing worked.

She yelled at the bird, and the bird got worse. She shook the bird, and the bird got madder and more rude. Finally in a moment of desperation, Mary put the parrot in the freezer to get a minute of peace.

For a few moments she heard the bird swearing, squawking kicking and screaming and then, suddenly there was absolute quiet. Mary was frightened that she might have actually hurt the bird and quickly opened the freezer door.

The parrot calmly stepped out onto Mary's extended arm and said: "I'm very sorry that I offended you with my language and my actions and I ask your forgiveness. I will endeavor to correct my behavior and I am sure it will never happen again."

Mary was astounded at the changes in the bird's attitude and was about to ask what had changed him, when the parrot continued, "May I ask what the chicken did?"

* * * *

A penguin is driving his car through Arizona when the car begins to smoke.
He pulls off the highway into a small town and pulls into a service station.
He asks the attending mechanic to take a look. While the mechanic is checking out his car, the penguin decides to walk around the small town.

He spots an ice cream parlor, and being a penguin, decides to enjoy some ice cream. He orders the biggest bowl of vanilla ice cream in the place and, having no arms, only fins, proceeds to get the ice cream all over his face and chest.

After finishing up, he proceeds back to the station, where the mechanic is up under the hood of his car. He calls out to the mechanic, who looks up and says "Looks like you blew a seal."

The penguin replies "No, no, it's only ice cream."

* * * *

An Irishman went to London for a visit to the zoo. While there, he saw a man with an elephant act. The man claimed the elephant could look at a person and tell that person's age. The Irishman was very skeptical and said so, in no uncertain terms. The man had the elephant look at a small boy and the elephant stamped its foot nine times.

"Is that right?" he asked the man.

"Oh yes," the boy said.

The Irishman was very loud, saying he did not belive that this was true. The man asked the elephant to tell the ages of several people, and each time the elephant stamped his foot and the people said he was correct.

The Irishman got even louder and more abusive toward the man. Finally, the man could take it no longer and wagered the Irishman that the elephant could look at him and tell him his age. The Irishman took him up on the wager. The elephant looked real close at the Irishman, turned around, raised his tail and cut wind like you wouldn't believe, turned back around and stomped his foot twice.

Where upon the Irishman stumbled back and with a sound of disbelief in his voice cried, "Be gabbers! He's right . . . Farty-two!"

* * * *

One day, in the great forest, a magical frog was walking down to a water hole. This forest was so big that the frog had never seen another animal in all his life. By chance, that day a bear was chasing after a rabbit to have for dinner.

The frog called for the two to stop. The frog said, "Because you are the only two animals I ever have seen, I will grant you both three wishes. Bear, you go first." The bear thought for a minute, and being the male he was, said, "I wish for all the bears in this forest, besides me, to be female."

For his wish, the rabbit asked for a crash helmet, and immediately put it on. The bear was amazed at the stupidity of the rabbit, wasting his wish like that.

It was the bear's second turn for a wish. "Well, I wish that all the bears in the next forest were female as well."

The rabbit asked for a motorcycle and immediately hopped on it and gunned the engine. The bear was shocked that the rabbit was asking for these stupid things. After all, he could have asked for money and bought the motorcycle.

For the last wish, the bear thought for awhile and then said, "I wish that all the bears in the world, besides me, were female."

The rabbit grinned, gunned the engine, and said, "I wish that the bear was gay."

* * * *

A vampire bat came flapping in from the night, face all covered in fresh blood and parked himself on the roof of the cave to get some sleep.

Pretty soon all the other bats smelt the blood and began hassling him about where he got it. He told them to piss off and let him get some sleep, but they persisted until he finally gave in.

"Okay, follow me," he said and flew out of the cave with hundreds of bats behind him. Down through a valley they went, across a river and into a huge forest. Finally he slowed down and all the other bats excitedly milled around him, tongues hanging out for blood.

"Do you see that large oak tree over there?" he asked.

"YES, YES, YES!!!!" the bats all screamed in a frenzy.

"Good!" said the first bat, "Because I fucking didn't."

* * * *

Police Officer George and Officer Mary had been assigned to walk the beat. They had only been out a short while when Mary said, "Damn, I was running late this morning and forgot to put on my panties! We have to go back to the station to get them."

George replied, "We don't have to go back. Just give Fido, my trusty police dog, one sniff, and he will go fetch them for you." It was a hot day and Mary didn't feel like heading back to the station, so she lifted her skirt for the dog. Fido's nose shoots between her legs, sniffing and snorting. After ten seconds of sniffing, Fido's ears pick up, he sniffs the wind, and he is off in a flash towards the station house.

Five minutes go by, and no sign of Fido. Ten minutes pass, and the dog is nowhere to be seen. Fifteen minutes pass, and they are starting to worry. Twenty minutes pass, and they hear sirens in the distance. The sirens get louder and louder. Suddenly, followed by a dozen police cars, Fido rounds the corner with the Desk Sergeant's balls in his mouth!

* * * *

A local business was looking for office help. They put a sign in the window, stating the following: "HELP WANTED. Must be able to type, must be good with a computer and must be bilingual. We are an Equal Opportunity Employer."

A short time afterwards, a dog trotted up to the window, saw the sign and went inside. He looked at the receptionist and wagged his tail, then walked over to the sign, looked at it and whined.

Getting the idea, the receptionist got the office manager. The office manager looked at the dog and was surprised, to say the least. However, the dog looked determined, so he led him into the office. Inside, the dog jumped up on the chair and stared at the manager. The manager said, "I can't hire you. The sign says you have to be able to type."

The dog jumped down, went to the typewriter and proceeded to type out a perfect letter. He took out the page and trotted over to the manager and gave it to him, then jumped back on the chair. The manager was stunned, but then told the dog, "The sign says you have to be good with a computer."

The dog jumped down again and went to the computer. The dog proceeded to enter and execute a perfect program, that worked flawlessly the first time.

By this time the manager was totally dumb-founded! He looked at the dog and said, "I realize that you are a very intelligent dog and have some interesting abilities. However, I *still* can't give you the job."

The dog jumped down and went to a copy of the sign and put his paw on the sentences that told about being an Equal Opportunity Employer.

The manager said, "Yes, but the sign *also* says that you have to be bilingual".

The dog looked at the manager calmly and said, "Meow."

* * * *

A wealthy old lady decides to go on a photo safari in Africa, taking her faithful aged poodle named Cuddles, along for the company. One day the poodle starts chasing butterflies and before long, Cuddles discovers that she's lost. Wandering about, she notices a leopard heading rapidly in her direction with the intention of having lunch. The old poodle thinks, "Oh, oh! I'm in deep doo-doo now!"

Noticing some bones on the ground close by, she immediately settles down to chew on the bones with her back to the approaching cat. Just as the leopard is about to leap, the old poodle exclaims loudly, "Boy, that was one delicious leopard! I wonder if there are any more around here?"

Hearing this, the young leopard halts his attack in mid-strike, a look of terror comes over him and he slinks away into the trees.

"Whew!" says the leopard, "That was close! That old poodle nearly had me!" Meanwhile, a monkey who had been watching the whole scene from a nearby tree, figures he can put this knowledge to good use and trade it for protection from the leopard. So off he goes, but the old poodle sees him heading after the leopard with great speed, and figures that something must be up. The monkey soon catches up with the leopard, spills the beans and strikes a deal for himself with the leopard. The young leopard is furious at being made a fool of and says, "Here, monkey, hop on my back and see what's going to happen to that conniving canine!"

Now, the old poodle sees the leopard coming with the monkey on his back and thinks, "What am I going to do now?" but instead of running, the dog sits down with her back to her attackers, pretending she hasn't seen them yet, and just when they get close enough to hear, the old poodle says, "Where's that damn monkey? I sent him off an hour ago to bring me another leopard!"

* * * *

There was a guy riding through the desert on his camel. He had been travelling so long that he felt the need to have sex. Obviously there were no women in the desert, so the man turned to his camel. He tried to position himself to have sex with his camel but the camel ran away. The man ran to catch up to the camel and got back on and started to ride again. Soon he was feeling the urge to have sex again so once again, he turned to his camel. The camel refused by running away. So he caught up to it again and got on it again.

Finally, after riding the camel through the whole desert the man came to a road. There was a broken down car with three big-chested beautiful blondes sitting in it. He went up to them and asked the women if they needed any help. The hottest girl said, "If you fix our car we will do anything you want." The man luckily knew a thing or two about cars and fixed it in a flash. When he finished, the three girls asked, "How could we ever repay you, mister?"

After thinking for a short while he replied, "Could you hold my camel?"

* * * *

The Taco Bell Chihuahua, a Doberman and a bulldog are in a bar having a drink when a great-looking female collie comes up to them and says, "Whoever can say liver and cheese in a sentence can have me."

So the Doberman says, "I love liver and cheese."

The collie replies, "That's not good enough."

The bulldog says, "I hate liver and cheese."

She says, "That's not creative enough."

Finally, the Chihuahua says, "Liver alone . . . cheese mine.

* * * *

A man takes his wife to a cattle stock show. They start heading down the alley that had the bulls.

They come up to the first bull and the sign states, "This bull mated 50 times last year."

The wife turns to her husband and says, "He mated fifty times last year. You could learn from him."

They proceed to the next bull and his sign states, "This bull mated 65 times last year."

The wife turns to her husband and says, "This bull mated 65 times last year. That's over 5 times a month. You could learn from him, also."

They proceed to the last bull and his sign states, "This bull mated 365 times last year."

The wife says, "Wow, he mated 365 times last year. That's once a day. You could really learn from him."

The husband turns to his wife and says, "Go up and ask if it was 365 times with the same cow."

* * * *

One evening, the old farmer decided to go down to the pond. He grabbed a five-gallon bucket to bring back some fruit. As he neared the pond, he heard voices shouting and laughing with glee. As he came closer he saw it was a bunch of young women skinny-dipping in his pond. He made the women aware of his presence, and they all went to the deep end. One of the women shouted to him, "We're not coming out until you leave!"

Think fast, the old man frowned, "I didn't come down here to watch you ladies swim naked or make you get out of the pond naked." Holding the bucket up, he said, "I'm here to feed the alligator."

* * * *

A fireman looked out of the firehouse window and noticed a little boy playing on the sidewalk. He had small ladders hung on the side of his little red wagon, and a garden hose coiled up in it. He was wearing a fireman's hat. He had the wagon tied to his dog so that the dog could pull the wagon. The fireman thought this was really cute, so he went out and told the little boy what a great-looking firetruck he had. As he did, he noticed that the dog was tied to the wagon by his testicles.

The fireman said, "Son, I don't want to tell you how to run your fire company or anything, but I think if you would tie that rope around the dog's neck you would go faster."

"Maybe so," said the little boy, "but then I'd lose my siren!"

* * * *

A farmer and his wife were lying in bed one evening. She was knitting, he was reading the latest issue of *Animal Husbandry.* He looks up from the page and says to her, "Did you know that humans are the only species in which the female achieves orgasm?"

She looks at him wistfully, smiles, and replies, "Oh yeah? Prove it."

He frowns for a moment, then says, "Okay."

He then gets up and walks out, leaving his wife with a confused look on her face. About a half an hour later he returns all tired and sweaty and proclaims, "Well I'm sure the cow and sheep didn't, but the way that pig's always squealing, how can I tell?"

* * * *

Two ducks go on their honeymoon and stay in a hotel. As they are about to make love, the male duck says, "Oh, we haven't got any condoms. I'll ring down to room service."

He calls and asks for some condoms. The woman says, "Okay sir, would you like to put them on your bill?"

"No," he says. "I'll suffocate!"

* * * *

Father, mother and son decide to go to the zoo one day. So they set off and are seeing lots of animals. Eventually they end up opposite the elephant house.

The boy looks at the elephant, sees its willie, points to it and says, "Mummy, what is that long thing?"

His mother replies, "That, son, is the elephant's trunk."

"No, at the other end."

"That, son, is the tail."

"No, mummy, the thing under the elephant."

A short embarrassed silence after which she replies, "That's nothing."

The mother goes to buy some ice-cream and the boy, not being satisfied with her answer, asks his father the same question. "Daddy, what is that long thing?"

"That's the trunk, son," replies the father.

"No, at the other end."

"Oh, that is the tail."

"No, no daddy, the thing below, " asks the son in desperation .

"That is the elephant's penis. Why do you ask son?"

"Well, Mummy said it was nothing," says the boy.

Replies the father, "Your mother is spoiled."

* * * *

A duck goes into a bar and asks, "Have you got any eggs?"

The bartender says, "This is a bar. We don't do eggs."

Next day, the duck comes back in and asks, "Have you got any eggs?"

The bartender says, "I told you yesterday we don't do eggs."

Next day, the duck comes back in and asks, "Have you got any eggs?"

The bartender says "I've had enough of you, if you come in here again and ask for eggs I'm gonna nail your fuckin' beak to the floor."

The next day the duck comes in and asks, "Have you got any nails?"

The bartender says, "NO!"

"Okay, have you got any eggs?"

* * * *

One day Jane met Tarzan in the jungle. She was very attracted to him and during her questions about his life, she asked him how he managed for sex.

"What's that?" he asked.

She explained to him what sex was, and he said, "Oh, Tarzan use hole in trunk of tree."

Horrified, she said, "Tarzan, you have it all wrong! I will show you how to do it properly."

She took off her clothes, laid down on the ground, and spread her legs. "Here," she said, pointing, "You must put it in here."

Tarzan removed his loincloth, stepped closer, and then gave her an almighty kick in the crotch. Jane screamed and rolled around in agony for several minutes.

Eventually, she managed to gasp, "What the hell did you do that for?"

"Tarzan always check for bees."

* * * *

Once there was a millionaire who collected live alligators. He kept them in a pool in the back of his mansion. The millionaire also had a beautiful daughter who was single.

One day, he decided to throw a huge party. During the party he announced, "My dear guests . . . I have a proposition to every man here. I will give one million dollars or my daughter to the man who can swim across this pool full of alligators and emerge alive!"

As soon as he finished his last word, there was the sound of a large *splash*! There was one guy in the pool swimming with all he could and screaming out of fear. The crowd cheered him on as he kept stroking as though he was running for his life. Finally he made it to the other side with only a torn shirt and some minor injuries. The millionaire was impressed. He said, "My boy, that was incredible! Fantastic! I didn't think it could be done! Well, I must keep my end of the bargain. Do you want my daughter or the one million dollars?"

The guy says, "Listen, I don't want your money, nor do I want your daughter! I want the person who pushed me into the water!"

* * * *

A successful Colorado cattle rancher died and left everything to his devoted wife. She was a very good-looking woman, and determined to keep the ranch, but knew very little about ranching. So she decided to place an ad in the newspaper for a ranch hand. Two men applied for the job. One was gay and the other a drunk. She thought long and hard about it, and when no one else applied she decided to hire the gay man, figuring it would be safer to have him around the house than the drunk.

He proved to be a hard worker who put in long hours everyday and knew a lot about ranching. For weeks, the two of them worked hard, and the ranch was doing very well. Then one day, the rancher's widow said to the hired hand, "You have done a really good job, and the ranch looks great! You should go into town and kick up your heels." The hired hand readily agreed and went into town the following Saturday night. One o'clock came, and he didn't return.

Two o'clock, and no hired hand.

He finally returned around two-thirty, and upon entering the house, he found the rancher's widow sitting by the fireplace with a glass of wine, waiting for him. She quietly called him over to her. "Unbutton my blouse and take it off," she said.

Trembling, he did as she directed. "Now take off my boots."

He did as she asked, ever so slowly. "Now take off my stockings."

He removed each gently and placed them neatly by her boots. "Now take off my skirt."

He slowly unbuttoned it, constantly watching her eyes in the fire light. "Now take off my bra."

Again, with trembling hands, he did as he was told and dropped it to the floor. "Now," she said, "take off my panties." By the light of the fire, he slowly pulled them down and off.

She looked at him and said, "If you ever wear my clothes into town again, you're fired."

* * * *

A woman pregnant with triplets was walking down the street when a masked robber ran out of a bank and shot her three times in the stomach. Luckily, the babies were okay. The surgeon decided to leave the bullets in because it was too risky to operate.

She gave birth to two healthy daughters and a healthy son. All was fine for 16 years, and then one day a daughter walked into the room in tears.

"What's wrong?" asked the mother.

"I was taking a tinkle and this bullet came out," replied the daughter.

The mother told her it was okay, and explained what happened 16 years ago.

About a week later the second daughter walks into the room in tears.

"Mom, I was taking a tinkle, and this bullet came out."

Again, the mother told her not to worry and explained what happened 16 years ago.

A week later her son walked into the room in tears. "It's okay" said the Mom, "I know what happened. You were taking a tinkle and a bullet came out."

"No," said the boy, "I was playing with myself and I shot the dog."

＊＊＊＊

Two aliens landed on a dairy farm. The farmer and his wife took the aliens in and showed them their way of life and everything. One day the farmer and his wife get to talking. The farmer asks his wife, "I wonder what the aliens do for sex?"

The farmer's wife replied, "I don't know. Do you want to find out?" The farmer agrees.

So, that night, the farmer took the female alien up to one room, while his wife took the male alien up to another room. As the wife was getting into bed, she looked down at the alien's pecker and starts laughing. "You've got to be kidding me!" she laughed.

The alien told her to wait for a moment. Then he slapped his cheeks and pulled his ears and the thing grew to a very impressive size. The next day, the farmer asks his wife, "So, how was your night?"

She replied, "Oh, it was wonderful. It was the best night of my life! How was yours?" "Well, not so good," replied the farmer, "all she kept doing all night was slapping my cheeks and pulling my ears."

＊＊＊＊

First-grade class in Brooklyn comes in from recess. Teacher asks Sarah: "What did you do at recess?"

Sarah says, "I played with the little mouse."

The teacher says, "That's good. Go to the blackboard, and if you can write 'little' correctly, I'll give you a fresh-baked cookie."

She does and gets a cookie.

The teacher asks Morris what he did at recess.

Morris says, "I played with Sarah and the mouse."

The teacher says, "Good. If you write 'mouse' correctly on the blackboard, I'll give you a fresh-baked cookie."

Morris does, and gets a cookie. Teacher then asks Mustaffa Abdul Makmoud what he did at recess.

He says, "I tried to play with Sarah and Morris, but they threw mouse poops at me."

The teacher says, "Threw mouse poops at you? That sounds like blatant racial discrimination. If you can go the blackboard and write 'blatant racial discrimination,' I'll give you a cookie."

* * * *

A young blonde was on vacation in the depths of Louisiana. She wanted a pair of genuine alligator shoes in the worst way, but was very reluctant to pay the high prices the local vendors were asking. After becoming very frustrated with the 'no haggle' attitude of one of the shopkeepers, the blonde shouted, "Maybe I'll just go out and catch my own alligator so I can get a pair of shoes at a reasonable price!"

The shopkeeper said, "By all means, be my guest. Maybe you'll luck out and catch yourself a big one!"

Determined, the blonde turned and headed for the swamps, set on catching herself an alligator. Later in the day, the shopkeeper is driving home, when he spots the young woman standing waist deep in the water, shotgun in hand.

Just then, he sees a huge 9-foot alligator swimming quickly toward her. She takes aim, kills the creature and with a great deal of effort, hauls it on to the swamp bank. Laying nearby were several more of the dead creatures.

The shopkeeper watches in amazement. Just then the blonde flips the alligator on it's back, and frustrated, shouts out, "Damn it, this one isn't wearing any shoes either!"

JOKE ANALYSIS
BY DR. BROWN

Comparisons are frequently drawn between humans and animals in the lexicon of story-based humor and well beyond. Working like a horse, swimming like a fish, fucking like a bunny, etc. Thus is seems appropriate that the following joke came to me courtesy of a fawn-like vixen with a Cheshire Cat grin and great tits.

The only cow in a small town in southern Minnesota stopped giving milk. The local farmers did some research and found that they could buy a cow from Iowa for 200 dollars, or one from Michigan for 100 dollars.

Being frugal Swedes, they bought the cow from Michigan. The cow was wonderful, producing lots of milk all the time, and the people were amazed and very happy.

The townspeople decided to acquire a bull to mate with the cow and produce more cows like this wonderful Michigan cow. Then they would never have to worry about their milk supply again. They bought a bull and put it in the pasture with their beloved cow. However, whenever the bull came close to the cow, the cow would move. No matter what approach the bull tried, the cow would just move away from the bull, and he could not succeed in his amorous quest.

The townspeople were very upset and decided to ask a local retired professor who was very wise in such complicated matters just what they should do. They told the professor what was happening.

"Whenever the bull approaches the cow, she moves away. If he approaches from the back, she moves forward. When he approaches her from the front, she moves to the back. An approach from the side and she just walks away to the other side."

The retired professor thought about this for a minute and then asked, "Did you buy this cow from Michigan?" The townspeople were dumbfounded, since they had never mentioned where they had gotten the cow.

"You are truly a wise professor," they said. "How did you know we got the cow from Michigan?"

The professor answered sagely, "My wife is from Michigan . . ."

While undoubtedly amusing, this joke suffers badly from improper stereotyping, as Swedes are hardly known for their frugality.

Rather these blond oafs from the North Country are known for a taciturn reserve that is so profound that it could almost pass for intelligence, were it not for their blank, blue-eyed stares and their love of cod soaked in lye.

Indeed, their silence turns out to be their greatest virtue, for should a Swede speak, he invariably speaks either of the utter futility of life, or worse, the joys of playing offensive line in high school.

The idea that Swedes could congregate together as "townspeople" stretches credulity to the limit, as Swedes are solitary by nature, and can usually only be found alone in a barn, morosely cleaning shotguns while drinking heavily.

Moreover, should a Swede confront a frustrating problem, he would never consult a professor. No. The true Swede would mull silently on the heifer's diffidence until finally one day, fueled by drink and years of bottled rage, he would solve the problem by throwing the cow into a wood-chipper.

Unfortunately in this case, solving the problem of improper stereotyping is no easy matter. Jews and Scotsmen are the traditional butt of jokes requiring frugality. But thanks to the addition of livestock, neither ethnicity works in this case. The only time a Jew would set foot near a farm is when his usurious bank was repossessing it. And as for a Scots village owning a cow — after being sodomized every day by lonely Scots farmers, any cow would long for the company of her own species.

And, when one factors in the fact that women from Michigan are all either white trailer trash who gladly turn tricks for crystal meth, or black women who like to fuck all night while their husbands work the third shift on the assembly line, or bored Grosse Pointe housewives who spend all their days on their knees servicing swarthy Latino pool boys, then one quickly realizes that a cow from Michigan will do most anything for hot cock, just so long as she's not married to it.

Therefore, while this joke may serve to amuse children and Poles, its glaring errors render it unusable for thinking audiences. As a substitute, I recommend "the pig and the cow" as more suitable for the discriminating palate:

A Jew, a Black and an Italian are stranded at a lonely farmhouse. The farmer explains that two of them can sleep in the farmhouse, but one of them must sleep in the barn with the pig and the cow.

The Jew volunteers, but after a moment he returns to the farmhouse, complaining that the stench of the pig offends his religion.

The Black goes out to the barn. After a while, there is a knock at the farmhouse door. It is the Black. He explains that he can stand the stench of the pig, but that the cow is too much for him.

The Italian then retires to the barn. After a moment, there is yet another knock on the door. Outside are the pig and the cow.

REL 315

RELIGION AND GENDER

Course:	REL 315 Religion and Gender
Semester:	Spring of even years
Credits:	3
Description:	The relationship between religion and gender viewed through foundational sacred texts and dusty know-it-alls that define gender, sexuality, the body, the divine. Contemporary responses to the relationship between religion and gender through ritual, liturgy, habit probing, burka baiting and the inter-frock scavenger hunting. Tardy class members will be condemned to a hoary netherworld.
Dates:	FALL - Open

Beyond being largely uneducated, unpopular and, as you must have gathered by now, crude, I am also godless. I wasn't raised with any kind of religion in my house and none of the external sources really impressed me much. But religious devotion does play a very important role in my life; it's the natural starting block for irreverence. What could possibly look gutsier to the devout than verbally mooning whatever God they fear? They enjoy the luxury of a good laugh at God's expense because someone else will be receiving eternal damnation for it. So, go forth my children and render unto those who worship these sacrilegious homilies.

I'll see you in hell.

—*Steve*

A man sits down in a church confessional, and says, "Forgive me, Father, for I have sinned, I slept with five different women last night."

The priest replies, "Go home, squeeze five lemons in a glass, and drink it all real fast."

"And I will be forgiven?" asks the man.

"No," replies the priest, "but it will wipe that fucking smirk off your face."

* * * *

A nun feels guilty and goes to confession. "Father, I seek absolution for my sins," she says. "I never wear panties under my habit."

"That's not so bad, sister," says the priest. "Just say five Hail Marys and five Our Fathers and then do five cartwheels."

* * * *

Twelve priests were about to be ordained. The final test was for them to line up in a straight row, totally naked, while a beautiful, big-breasted nude model danced before them.

Each priest had a small bell attached to his penis. They were told that anyone whose bell rang when the nude model danced in front of them would not be ordained, because he had not reached a state of spiritual purity.

The beautiful model danced before the first candidate, with no reaction. She proceeded down the line with the same response from all the priests until she got to the final priest. As she danced, his bell began to ring so loudly that it flew off and fell clattering to the ground. Embarrassed, he took a few steps forward and bent over to pick up the bell.

Then all the other bells started to ring.

* * * *

They all find themselves at the pearly gates waiting to enter Heaven. On entering they must present something "Christmassy" to show they remember the holiday, or off to hell they go. The first man searches his pocket, and finds some Mistletoe, so he is allowed in. The second man presents a candy cane, so he too is allowed in. The third man pulls out a pair of panties. Confused at this last gesture, St. Peter asks, "How do these represent Christmas?"

"They're Carol's."

* * * *

A nun is sitting with her Mother Superior chatting. "I used some horrible language this week and feel absolutely terrible about it." said the younger nun.

"When did you use this awful language?" asks the elder nun.

"Well, I was golfing and hit an incredible drive that looked like it was going to go over 280 yards, but it struck a phone line that was hanging over the fairway and fell straight down to the ground after going only about 100 yards."

"Is that when you swore?"

"No, Mother," answered the nun. "After that, a squirrel ran out of the bushes and grabbed my ball in its mouth and began to run away."

"Is THAT when you swore?" asks the Mother Superior again.

"Well, no," says the nun. "You see, as the squirrel was running, an eagle came down out of the sky, grabbed the squirrel in his talons and began to fly away!"

"And Is THAT when you swore?" asks the amazed elder nun.

"No, not yet." she answered. "As the eagle carried the squirrel away in its claws, it flew near the green and the squirrel dropped my ball."

"Did you swear THEN?" asked Mother Superior, becoming impatient.

"No, because the ball fell on a big rock, bounced over the sand trap, rolled onto the green, and stopped about six inches from the hole."

The two nuns were silent for a moment.

Then Mother Superior sighed and said, "You missed the fucking putt, didn't you?"

* * * *

Everybody on Earth dies and goes to heaven. God comes and says, "I want the men to make two lines, one line for the men who dominated their women on earth and the other line for the men who were dominated by their women. Also, I want all the women to go with Gabriel."

Said and done.

The next time God looked the women were gone, and there were two lines. The line of the men who were dominated by their women was 100 miles long, and in the line of men who dominated their women, there was only one man.

God got mad and said, "You men should be ashamed of yourselves. I created you in my image and you were all whipped by your spouses. Look at the only one man that stood up and made me proud. Learn from him! Tell them my man, how did you manage to be the only one in this line?"

The man replied, "I don't know. My girlfriend told me to stand here."

* * * *

Seems God was just about done creating the universe, had a couple of left-over things left in his bag of creations, so he stopped by to visit Adam and Eve in the Garden. He told the couple that one of the things he had to give away was the ability to stand up and pee. "It's a very handy thing," God told the couple who he found hanging around under an apple tree. "I was wondering if either one of you wanted that ability."

Adam popped a cork, jumped up and begged, "Oh, give that to me! I'd love to be able to do that! It seems the sort of thing a man should do. Oh please, oh please, oh please, let me have that ability. It would be so great! When I'm working in the garden or naming the animals, I could just let it rip, I'd be so cool. Oh please God let it be me who you give that gift to, let me stand and pee, oh please . . ."

On and on he went like an excited little boy (who had to pee).

Eve just smiled and shook her head at the display. She told God that if Adam really wanted it so badly, and it sure seemed to be the sort of thing that would make him happy, she really wouldn't mind if Adam were the one given the ability to stand up and pee. And so it was. And it was . . . well, good.

"Fine," God said, looking back into His bag of left-over gifts. "And what do we have left here? Oh yes, multiple orgasms . . ."

* * * *

God creates Adam, and soon Adam is complaining that he's all alone in the Garden of Eden. So God says, "Okay, I'll make you a companion, a beautiful creature who'll cook and clean for you. It will be able to converse intelligently on any subject, and never ever complain or argue."

Adam says, "That sounds great."

God says, "The only thing is, it will cost you an arm and a leg."

Adam says, "Damn, that's expensive. What can I get for a rib?"

* * * *

Two men waiting at the pearly gates strike up a conversation. "How'd you die?" the first man asks the second. "I froze to death," says the second.

"That's awful. How does it feel to freeze to death?" says the first.

"It's very uncomfortable at first. You get the shakes, and you get pains in all your fingers and toes. But eventually, it's a very calm way to go. You get numb and you kind of drift off, as if you're sleeping. How did you die?" says the second.

"I had a heart attack," says the first guy. "You see, I knew my wife was cheating on me, so one day I showed up at home unexpectedly. I ran up to the bedroom, and found her alone, knitting. I ran down to the basement, but no one was hiding there. I ran up to the second floor, but no one was hiding there either. I ran as fast as I could to the attic, and just as I got there, I had a massive heart attack and died."

The second man shakes his head. "That's so ironic," he says.

"What do you mean?" asks the first man.

"If you had only stopped to look in the freezer, we'd both still be alive."

* * * *

Arthur Davidson died and went to heaven. At the gates, St. Peter told Arthur, "Since you've been such a good man and your motorcycles have changed the world, your reward is that you can hang out with anyone you want in Heaven."

Arthur thought about it for a minute and then said, "I want to hang out with God." St. Peter took Arthur to the Throne Room and introduced him to God.

God recognized Arthur and commented, "Okay, so you were the one who invented the Harley Davidson motorcycle?"

Arthur said, "Yep, that's me."

God said, "Well, what's the big deal in inventing something that's pretty unstable, makes noise and pollution, and can't run without a road?"

Arthur was apparently embarrassed, but finally he said, "Excuse me, but aren't you the inventor of woman?"

God said, "Yes."

"Well," said Arthur, "professional to professional, you have some major design flaws in your invention:

1. There's too much inconsistency in the front-end protrusions;

2. It chatters constantly at high speeds;

3. Most of the rear ends are too soft and wobble too much;

4. The intake is placed way too close to the exhaust;

5. And the maintenance costs are enormous!"

"Hmmmmm, you have some good points there," replied God. "Hold on." God went to His Celestial Supercomputer, typed in a few words and waited for the results. The computer printed out a slip of paper and God read it. "Well, it may be true that my invention is flawed," God said to Arthur, "but according to these numbers, more men are riding my invention than yours."

* * * *

A priest, a Pentecostal preacher and a Rabbi all served as chaplains to the students of Northern Michigan University in Marquette. They would get together two or three times a week for coffee and to talk shop.

One day, someone made the comment that preaching to people isn't really all that hard. A real challenge would be to preach to a bear. One thing led to another, and they decided to do an experiment. They would all go out into the woods, find a bear, preach to it, and attempt to convert it.

Seven days later, they all got together to discuss the experience. Father Flannery, who has his arm in a sling, is on crutches and has various bandages, goes first. "Well," he says, "I went into the woods to find me a bear. And when I found him I began to read to him from the Catechism. Well, that bear wanted nothing to do with me and began to slap me around. So I quickly grabbed my holy water, sprinkled him and, Holy Mary Mother of God, he became as gentle as a lamb. The bishop is coming out next week to give him first communion and confirmation."

Reverend Billy Bob spoke next. He was in a wheelchair, with an arm and both legs in casts, and an IV drip. In his best fire and brimstone oratory he claimed, "WELL brothers, you KNOW that we don't sprinkle! I went out and I FOUND me a bear. And then I began to read to my bear from God's HOLY WORD! But that bear wanted nothing to do with me. So I took HOLD of him and we began to wrestle. We wrestled down one hill, UP another and DOWN another until we came to a creek. So I quickly DUNKED him and BAPTIZED his hairy soul. And just like you said, he became as gentle as a lamb. We spent the rest of the day praising Jesus."

They both looked down at the rabbi, who was lying in a hospital bed. He was in a body cast and traction with IV's and monitors running in and out of him. He was in bad shape. The rabbi looks up and says, "Looking back on it, circumcision may not have been the best way to start."

* * * *

Brother John entered the 'Monastery of Silence,' and the Chief Priest said, "Brother, this is a silent monastery. You are welcome here as long as you like, but you may not speak until I direct you to do so."

Brother John lived in the monastery for a full year before the Chief Priest said to him, "Brother John, you have been here a year now, you may speak two words."

Brother John said, "Hard bed."

"I'm sorry to hear that," the Chief Priest said. "We will get you a better bed."

The next year, Brother John was called by the Chief Priest. "You may now say another two words, Brother John."

"Cold food." said Brother John. The Chief Priest assured him that the food would be better in the future.

On his third anniversary at the monastery, the Chief Priest again called Brother John into his office. "Two words you may say today, Brother John."

"I quit," said Brother John.

"It is probably for the best," said the Chief Priest. "All you have done since you got here is complain."

* * * *

If college students wrote the Bible:
The Last Supper would have been eaten the next morning - cold.
The Ten Commandments would actually be only five, double-spaced and written in a large font.
New edition would be published every two years in order to limit reselling.
Forbidden fruit would have been eaten because it wasn't cafeteria food.
Paul's letter to the Romans would become Paul's email to abuse@romans.gov.
Reason Cain killed Abel: They were roommates.
Reason why Moses and followers walked in the desert for 40 years: They didn't want to ask directions and look like freshmen.
Instead of God creating the world in six days and resting on the seventh, He would have put it off until the night before it was due and then pulled an all-nighter.

* * * *

A man appeared before St. Peter at the pearly gates. "Have you ever done anything of particular merit?" St. Peter asked.

"Well, I can think of one thing," the man offered. "Once, on a trip to the Black Hills of South Dakota, I came upon a gang of high-testosterone bikers who were threatening a young woman. I directed them to leave her alone, but they wouldn't listen. So, I approached the largest and most heavily tattooed biker and smacked him on the head, kicked his bike over, ripped out his nose ring and threw it on the ground. I yelled, 'Now back off, biker boy, or you'll answer to me!'"

St. Peter was impressed. "When did this happen?" he asked.

"Just a couple of minutes ago."

* * * *

Two nuns are hard at work painting the monastery. It is very, very hot and one nun says to the other, "Do you think it would be evil if we took our habits off since we're working so hard and it's so hot?" The other nun said, "Well, we're all alone and no one ever comes here to the monastery, so it will be fine."

So the nuns took their habits off and were painting in the nude when all of a sudden, a knock was heard at the door. "Who's there?" they cried in a panic.

"The blind man," came the reply.

"Well," said the first nun, "if he is blind, it won't make any difference."

So the nuns opened the door.

"Nice tits!" said the man. "Where do you want me to put the blinds?"

* * * *

Einstein is walking through heaven one day, when St. Peter approaches him. "Albert, my friend." he says. "I have some pressing business with Jesus, and I was wondering if you might watch the gate for a few minutes."

"Of course Peter," Einstein replies, "It would be my pleasure."

So Einstein takes over at the gate and as he is paging through the great book of souls, a man approaches the gate. "Welcome to Heaven." Einstein says, "I see here in the book that you are free to pass through the gates, but before you do, and if you don't mind my asking, what is your IQ?"

"I don't mind at all, Professor. My IQ is 200," the man replies.

"Excellent," Einstein says, "would you like to help me complete my grand unified field theory?"

"Of course Professor, it would be an honor."

"Good, but as you can see, I am watching the gate for St. Peter. If you would just wait inside, I'll be along in a few minutes."

The man passes into heaven, and presently a woman approaches the gates. Einstein greets her warmly, and in similar fashion, asks the woman her IQ. "Oh, I'm not sure, I never had it tested, but if I had to guess, I'd say around 180 or 190," she answers.

"Marvelous," Einstein beams. "Well, if you wouldn't mind, another gentleman and I are planning to work on my unfinished theories. If you would like to help, would you be so kind as to wait inside the gates for me, I'll be along in a few minutes."

"That would be wonderful, Dr. Einstein." The woman smiles and enters the gates.

A few moments later, another man approaches the gate, and again Einstein greets the man, asking him his IQ. "Oh, probably 70 or 80," the man replies.

"Ahhh," Einstein smiles, "How about those Denver Broncos?"

* * * *

Three men, a philosopher, a mathematician, and an idiot, were riding in a car when it crashed into a tree. Before they knew it, the three men found themselves standing at the pearly gates of Heaven, where St. Peter and the devil were standing nearby.

"Gentlemen," the devil started. "Due to the fact that Heaven is now overcrowded, St. Peter has agreed to limit the number of people entering Heaven. If anyone of you can ask me a question which I don't know or cannot answer, then you're worthy enough to go to Heaven. If not, then you'll come with me to Hell."

The philosopher then stepped up. "OK, give me the most comprehensive report on Socrates' teachings." With a snap of his fingers, a stack of paper appeared next to the devil. The philosopher read it and concluded it was correct.

"Then, go to Hell." With another snap of the devil's fingers, the philosopher disappeared.

The mathematician then asked, "Give me the most complicated formula you can ever think of." With a snap of his fingers, another stack of paper appeared next to the devil. The mathematician read it, and reluctantly agreed it was correct.

"Then go to Hell." With another snap of the devil's fingers, the mathematician disappeared too.

The idiot then stepped forward and said, "Bring me a chair." The devil brought forward a chair.

"Drill 7 holes on the seat." The devil did just that. The idiot then sat on the chair and let out a very loud fart. Standing up, he asked, "Which hole did my fart come out from?"

The devil inspected the seat and said, "The third hole from the right."

"Wrong," said the idiot. "It's from my asshole."

And the idiot went to Heaven.

* * * *

Biff and Bob were in an accident and killed instantly. Upon Biff's arrival to the pearly gates, he is met by St. Peter. "Where is my friend Bob?" asked Biff.

St. Peter replied, "Well Bob was not as fortunate as you. He went in the other direction instead of getting into heaven."

Biff was bothered by this, and asked, "Well, could I see Bob one more time just to make sure he's okay?" St. Peter agreed, so they walked to the edge of heaven and looked down. There was Bob, on a sandy beach, with a gorgeous, sexy blonde in a bikini and a keg of beer.

"I don't mean to complain, but Bob seems to have it pretty nice down there in Hell," said Biff.

"It's not as it appears to be," said St. Peter. "You see, the keg has a hole in it, and the blonde doesn't."

* * * *

The Pope and the Queen of England are on the same stage in front of a huge crowd. Her Majesty and His Holiness, however, have seen it all before. So to make it a little more interesting, the Queen says to the Pope, "Did you know that with just one little wave of my hand, I can make every English person in the crowd go wild?" He doubts it, so she shows him.

Sure enough, the royal-gloved wave elicits rapture and cheering from every English person in the crowd. Gradually, the cheering subsides.

The Pope, not wanting to be outdone by someone wearing a frock and hat worse than his, considers what he could do. "Your Majesty, that was impressive. But did you know that with just one little wave of MY hand, I can make every IRISH person in the crowd go crazy with joy? This joy will not be a momentary display like that of your subjects, but will go deep into their hearts, and they will forever speak of this day and rejoice."

The Queen seriously doubts this, and says so. "One little wave of your hand, and all Irish people will rejoice forever? Show me."

So, the Pope slapped her.

* * * *

An Irishman walks into a bar in Dublin, orders three pints of Guinness and sits in the back of the room, drinking a sip out of each one in turn. When he finishes them, he comes back to the bar and orders three more. The bartender approaches and tells him, "You know, a pint goes flat after I draw it. It would taste better if you bought one at a time."

The Irishman replies, "Well, you see, I have two brothers. One is in America, the other in Australia, and I'm here in Dublin. When we all left home, we promised that we'd drink this way to remember the days when we drank together. So I drinks one for each o' me brothers and one for me self."

The bartender admits that this is a nice custom, and leaves it there. The Irishman becomes a regular in the bar, and always drinks the same way: He orders three pints and drinks them in turn.

One day, he comes in and orders two pints. The other regulars take notice and fall silent. When he comes back to the bar for the second round, the bartender says, "I don't want to intrude on your grief, but I wanted to offer my condolences on your loss."

The Irishman looks confused for a moment, then his eyes light up and he laughs. "Oh no, everyone's fine," he explains. "It's just that I joined the Baptist Church and had to quit drinking."

* * * *

Two men, sentenced to die in the electric chair on the same day, were led down to the room in which they would meet their maker. The priest had given them last rites, the formal speech had been given by the warden, and a final prayer had been said among the participants. The warden, turning to the first man, solemnly asked, "Son, do you have a last request?"

The man replied, "Yes sir, I do. I love dance music. Could you please play the Macarena for me one last time?"

"Certainly," replied the warden.

He turned to the other man and asked, "Well, what about you, son? What is your final request?"

"Please," said the condemned man, "kill me first."

* * * *

One afternoon, three altar boys were standing outside in the snow with their pants down around their ankles. They all have placed their penises in a snow bank.

Sister Margaret sticks her head out the window and yells down to them, "Boys! Boys! Whatever are you doing? You're going to catch pneumonia. Put your penises away right this minute."

The tallest altar boy turned around and yelled back, "Sister Margaret, don't worry. We know what we're doing. Father Simpson always likes a couple cold ones after work."

* * * *

A thermodynamics professor wrote a take home exam for his graduate students. It had one question: 'Is hell exothermic or endothermic? Support your answer with proof. Most of the students wrote proofs of their beliefs using Boyle's Law or some variant.

One student, however, wrote the following:

First, we postulate that if souls exist, then they must have some mass. If they do, then a mole of souls can also have a mass. So, at what rate are souls moving into hell and at what rate are souls leaving? I think that we can safely assume that once a soul gets to hell, it will not leave. Therefore, no souls are leaving. As for souls entering hell, let's look at the religions that exist in the world today. Many religions state that if you are not a member of their religion, you will go to hell. Since there are more than one of these religions and people do not belong to more than one religion, we can project that all people and all souls go to hell. With birth and death rates as they are, we can expect the number of souls in hell to increase exponentially.

Now, we look at the rate of change in volume in hell. Boyle's Law states that in order for the temperature and pressure in hell to stay the same, the ratio of the mass of souls and volume needs to stay constant.

1. So, if hell is expanding at a slower rate than the rate at which souls enter hell, then the temperature and pressure in hell will increase until all hell breaks loose.

2. If hell is expanding at a rate faster than the increase of souls in hell, than the temperature and pressure will drop until hell freezes over.

So which is it? If we accept the postulate given me by Therese Banyan during freshman year, and take into account the fact that I still have not succeeded in having sexual relations with her, then #2 cannot be true, and hell is exothermic.'

****

A woman is standing in line at the pearly gates talking to St. Peter when she hears an awful scream. "What was that!?" she asks.

"Oh don't worry," St. Peter replies, "That was the person before you getting the holes drilled in their back for their wings."

"Ouch," she blurts.

Again she hears another ear-shattering scream. "Now what was that?" she inquires.

St. Peter responds, "The same person was getting holes drilled in their head for a halo." Terrified, the woman looks St. Peter in the eyes and says, "I think I'd rather go to hell."

He responds, "No, no, you don't want to do that. You'll be raped and sodomized there!"

The woman pauses and replies, "Well, at least I already have the holes for that!"

JOKE ANALYSIS
BY DR. BROWN

Given, as we assume they are, to aspirations of purity and ascetic leanings that would preclude expressions of jollity, it is always awkward to be regaled with a joke from a member of the clergy. Occasionally, one will even find a man of the cloth who fancies himself a cut up. Such is the case with Father Jack. There is no doubt that he retains more mirth and verse. Even more discomfiting is his reliance on blue material when his "A" stuff tanks. Here we examine his go-to bit.

Mr. O'Malley, a tall, red-headed Irishman; Mr. Goldstein, a short, stocky Jew; and Mr. Johnson, a thin, black man, are all waiting in the maternity ward lobby pacing the floor. The doctor comes in and calls them all over.

He says, "Gentlemen, I have great news. You are all the fathers of healthy baby boys. All of the mothers are doing fine. We do have one slight problem, however. As these babies were born at the exact same moment, with all of the commotion we have mixed up your sons."

The doctor then tells them that their fatherly instincts will guide them to their sons so one at a time they are directed to the nursery to pick out their sons.

Mr. O'Malley returns, having gone first, holding a blanket wrapped child and cooing to it tenderly. The doctor, pleased with his solution moves closer for a look and sees that the child is as black as coal.

He looks at O'Malley and says "Sir, you are red headed and pale, your wife is as fair as you, this can not be your son. What are you up to?"

O'Malley simply says, "I didn't want to take a chance on the Jew."

Alas, the mere concrescence of ethnicities does not guarantee humor. For a joke to work, it must maintain some connection to reality. Yet here, Father Jack would have us believe that an Irishman awaiting the birth of his child would be sober enough to speak coherently.

If that's not outrageous enough, Father Jack then asks us to imagine a world where a Black father-to-be is actually within miles of the delivery room. What next, one wonders: a non-drunken Indian? An Arab who smells good? A priest who likes women?

No. Far more preposterous, Father Jack actually expects us to believe that the Jew in question wouldn't be found leering over the Irish baby, siphoning off its pure, virgin Christian blood for his own unholy ceremonies.

Sure, its nice to imagine a fantasy world where trees are made of licorice and the moon is actually a friendly, talking marshmallow easily reachable by hot-air balloon. But we don't. And until the Teletubbies rule the earth with their plushy fists, we never will.

OST 535
PRINCIPLES OF
GERIATRICS

Course:	OST 535 Principles of Geriatrics
Semester:	Summer of every year
Credits:	2
Restrictions:	Open to graduate-professional students in the College of Osteopathic Medicine or in the College of Grumpy Cantankory or approval of department.
Description:	Lectures, readings, tapes, small group seminars, and home visits related to normal aging epidemiology. Major chronic diseases, hording of tasteless candies and the organic creation of mothball-like odors as well as other issues of geriatric care.
Dates:	SUMMER - Open

Ultimately, if we are lucky, we will all get old. Of course, there are matters of genetics that will dictate the rate of our decline, but it's still unlikely to be pretty. Assuming I'm a few years older than you already, I would like to pass along a word of advice: briefs. I know boxers look cool sticking out of the top of your pants, but your balls are like an oracle; a pair of magic eight balls that hold the story of your future and believe me, it's not photogenic.

—*Steve*

An older couple, both 67, went to a sex therapist's office.

The doctor asked, "What can I do for you?"

The man said, "Will you watch us have sexual intercourse?" The doctor looked puzzled, but agreed. The doctor examined them and then directed them to disrobe and go at it.

When the couple finished, the doctor reexamined them and, upon completion, advised the couple, "there's nothing wrong with the way you have intercourse."

He then charged them $32. This happened several weeks in a row. The couple would make an appointment, have intercourse with no apparent problems other than the lack of vigor which is to be expected in 67 year olds, get dressed, pay the doctor, and then leave.

Finally after almost two months of this routine, the doctor asked, "Just exactly what are you trying to find out?"

The old man said, "Oh, we're not trying to find out anything. She's married and we can't go to her house. I'm married, so we can't go to my house. The Holiday Inn charges $60. The Hilton charges $78. We do it here for $32, and I get $28 back from Medicare."

* * * *

A crusty old Sergeant Major found himself at a gala event, hosted by a local liberal arts college. There was no shortage of extremely young, idealistic ladies in attendance, one of whom approached the Sergeant Major for conversation.

She said, "Excuse me, Sergeant Major, but you seem to be a very serious man. Is something bothering you?"

"Negative, ma'am," the Sergeant Major said. "I am just serious by nature."

The young lady looked at his awards and decorations and said, "It looks like you have seen a lot of action."

The Sergeant Major's short reply was, "Yes, ma'am, a lot of action."

The young lady, tiring of trying to start up a conversation, said, "You know, you should lighten up a little. Relax and enjoy yourself."

The Sergeant Major just stared at her in his serious manner. Finally the young lady said, "You know, I hope you don't take this the wrong way, but when is the last time you had sex?"

The Sergeant Major looked at her and replied, "1955." She said, "Well, there you are. You really need to chill out and quit taking everything so seriously! I mean, no sex since 1955! She took his hand and led him to a private room where she proceeded to "relax" him several times. Afterwards, and panting for breath she leaned against his bare chest and said, "Wow, you sure didn't forget much since 1955!" The Sergeant Major, glancing at his watch, said in his matter-of-fact voice, "I hope not. It's only 2130 now."

* * * *

An old man and his wife have gone to bed. After laying there a few minutes the old man farts and says, "Seven points!"

His wife rolls over and says, "What in the world was that?"

The old man replied, "It's fart football."

A few minutes later the wife lets one go and says, "Touchdown, tie score."

After about five minutes, the old man farts again and says, "Touchdown, I'm ahead 14 to 7."

Not to be outdone, the wife rips another one and says, "Touchdown, tie score."

Five seconds go by and she lets out a squeaker and says, "Field goal, I lead 17 to 14."

Now the pressure's on and the old man refuses to get beaten by a woman so he strains real hard but to no avail. Realizing a defeat is totally unacceptable he gives it everything he has, but instead of farting, he shits the bed. The wife looks and says, "What the hell was that?"

The old man replied, "Half-time, Switch sides!"

* * * *

A rich old woman is dying and wants her daughter to take her chrome-plated .38 revolver so that she can always remember her mother.

"But Mummy, I really don't like guns. How about leaving me your Rolex watch instead?"

"My dear daughter, listen to me, you are going to take over my business, get a handsome husband and earn lot of money. One day, you may come home late and find your husband having sex with a bitch on the bed. What do you do then? Point to your watch and say, 'Time's up?'"

* * * *

Two old people, a man and a woman, walk into a hospital. The doctor says to the old man, "I'll need a urine sample, a feces sample, and a blood sample." The old man says, "What?"

So the doctor says it again. Once again the old man says, "What?"

So the doctor yells it, "I NEED A URINE SAMPLE, A FECES SAMPLE, AND A BLOOD SAMPLE!"

With that, the old woman turns to the old man and says, "He needs a pair of your underwear!"

* * * *

An 80 year old woman was arrested for shoplifting. When she went before the judge he asked her, "What did you steal?"

She replied, "a can of peaches."

The judge asked her why she had stolen them and she replied, "I was hungry."

The judge then asked her how many peaches were in the can. "Six," she replied.

The judge then said, "I will give you six days in jail."

Before the judge could actually pronounce the punishment, the woman's husband spoke up and asked the judge if he could say something.

The husband said, "She also stole a can of peas."

* * * *

Three old guys are sitting on a porch in Miami. Suddenly the first sighs and says, "Gentlemen, isn't life horrible. Here I am at an age that I can afford the best steaks, and what? Bad teeth and gums. I have to eat ground or soft foods."

The second answers, "Yeah, life is a real bummer. Why here I am at an age where I can buy the finest wine and champagne, but what? Ulcers, I have to drink milk."

The third sighs loudly and adds, "Gentlemen, I know exactly what you mean. Last night at 2 a.m., I nudged my wife and asked her if she was interested. She screamed at me, 'What is wrong with you dear? We just got finished doing it for the second time tonight!'

After a long pause the first man says, "So what is your problem?"

The third one grunts and says, "Can't you see? I'm losing my memory."

* * * *

A crusty old man walks into a bank and says to the teller, "I want to open a fucking checking account."

The astonished woman replies, "I beg your pardon, sir. I must have misunderstood you. What did you say?"

"Listen up. Damn it. I said I want to open a fucking checking account now!"

"I'm very sorry sir, but that kind of language is not tolerated in this bank."

The teller leaves the window and goes over to the bank manager to inform him of her situation. The manager agrees that the teller does not have to listen to that foul language.

They both return to the window, and the manager asks the old geezer, "Sir, what seems to be the problem here? "

"There is no damn problem," the man says. "I just won $200 million bucks in the fucking lottery and I want to put my fucking money in the damn bank."

"I see," says the manager, "and is this cunt giving you a hard time?"

* * * *

A old man was brought before the judge and charged with necrophilia — making love to a dead woman. The judge told him, "In 20 years on the bench, I've never heard such a disgusting, immoral thing. Just give me one good reason why I shouldn't lock you up and throw away the key!"

The man replied, "I'll give you THREE good reasons:

#1. It's none of your damn business

#2. She was my wife and . . .

#3. I didn't KNOW she was dead. She ALWAYS acted that way in bed!"

* * * *

An Irish woman "of a certain age" visited her doctor to ask his help in reviving her husband's sex drive.

"What about trying Viagra?" asks the doctor.

"Not a chance," she said. "He won't even take an aspirin."

"Not a problem," replied the doctor. "Drop it into his coffee. He won't even taste it. Give it a try and call me in a week to let me know how things went."

A week later she rang up the doctor, who directly inquired as to progress.

The poor dear exclaimed, "Oh, faith, bejaysus and begorrah! 'Twas horrid. Just terrible!"

"Really? What happened?" asked the doctor.

"Well, I did as you advised and slipped it in his coffee, didn't I? The effect was almost immediate. He jumped hisself straight up, with a twinkle in his eye, and with his pants a-bulging fiercely! With one swoop of his arm, he sent the cups and tablecloth flying, ripped me clothes to tatters and took me then and there, making wild, mad, passionate love to me on the tabletop! It was a nightmare, I tell you!"

"Why so terrible?" asked the doctor. "Do you mean you didn't enjoy it?"

"Of course I did doctor! Indeed, 'twas the best sex I've had in 25 years. But I'll never be able to show me face in Starbucks again."

* * * *

An elderly couple finally realized that a small pension and Social Security would not pay all their bills. The old man decided that his wife would have to work the streets to make a little extra cash. She agreed, a little excitedly, and went out on Saturday night to seek her fortune. When she came in exhausted on Sunday morning, her husband asked breathlessly how much money she had made. She replied, "Twenty-five dollars and five cents."

He was outraged. "Twenty-five oh five? Who gave you a nickel?"

She just smiled and said, "Everybody."

* * * *

Two 90 year olds had been dating for a while, when the man told the woman, "Well, tonight's the night we have sex!" And so they did. As they are lying in bed afterward, the man thinks to himself, "My God, if I knew she was a virgin, I would have been much gentler with her!"

And the woman was thinking to herself, "My God, if I knew the old fuck could actually get it up, I would have taken off my panty hose!"

An elderly woman went to the hospital and asked for genital reduction surgery. The surgeon assured her that it could be done. So she made the surgeon swear to keep this under total secrecy. When she regained consciousness after the surgery, she saw three red roses . She fumed. "I TOLD YOU NOT TO TELL ANYONE OF MY PUSSY SHRINKING PROCEDURE!!!"

The surgeon assured her he hadn't. The 1st rose is from me, the 2nd rose is from the nurse as she assisted me in the surgery and the 3rd rose is from a patient in the burns unit on the upper level thanking you for his new ears.

* * * *

An old cowboy sat down at the bar and ordered a drink. As he sat sipping his drink, a young woman sat down next to him. She turned to the cowboy and asked, "Are you a real cowboy?"

He replied, "Well, I've spent my whole life breaking colts, working cows, going to rodeos, fixing fences, pulling calves, bailing hay, doctoring calves, cleaning my barn, fixing flats, working on tractors, and feeding my dogs, so I guess I am a cowboy."

She said, "I'm a lesbian. I spend my whole day thinking about women. As soon as I get up in the morning, I think about women. When I shower, I think about women. When I watch TV, I think about women. I even think about women when I eat. It seems that everything makes me think of women."

The two sat sipping in silence. A little while later, a man sat down on the other side of the old cowboy and asked, "Are you a real cowboy?"

He replied, "I always thought I was, but I just found out I'm a lesbian."

* * * *

A mortician was working late one night. He examined the body of Old Man Schwartz, about to be cremated, and made a startling discovery. Schwartz had the largest private part he had ever seen! "I'm sorry Mr. Schwartz, "the mortician commented, "I can't allow you to be cremated with such an impressive private part. It must be saved for posterity." So, he removed it, stuffed it into his briefcase, and took it home.

"I have something to show you won't believe," he said to his wife, opening his briefcase.

"My God!" the wife exclaimed, "Schwartz is dead!"

* * * *

An old man's son decides to put him in a nursing home. The old man isn't happy about it but knows he can't look after himself as well as he used to, so the old man figures he'll spend as least one night in the home to give in a try.

The next morning he wakes up with a hard on. Out of nowhere a beautiful blonde nurse comes in and immediately starts giving him a blowjob. The old man can't believe his luck. He gets on the phone and calls his son. The old man says "Son thank you for putting me in here. I woke up with a hard on this morning and a beautiful nurse came in and gave me the best blowjob of my life.

The son says "See dad, that place isn't so bad now is it?"

Later that afternoon the old man is out taking a stroll with his walker and trips and falls. Out of nowhere this huge, ugly, hillbilly orderly comes and fucks him in the ass. The old man is freaked out. He calls his son and says, "Son, get me the hell out of here. I was out taking a walk and tripped and fell. Then this huge ugly, hillbilly orderly came and fucked me in the ass."

The son says "Well dad, you just got a blowjob this morning. You got to take the good with the bad."

The old man says, "No, son, you don't understand. I get a hard-on once a month. I trip and fall three or four times a day."

* * * *

An 80-year-old man goes to his doctor for his annual check-up. The doctor asks him how he's feeling. The 80-year-old says, "I've never felt better. I now have a bride so young she's still in college, and she is pregnant with my child. What do you think about that?"

The doctor considers his question for a minute and then begins.

"I have an older friend, much like you, who is an avid trophy hunter and never misses a season. One day, when he was going out hunting, he was in a bit of a hurry and accidentally picked up his walking cane instead of his gun. When he got to the creek, he saw a prime beaver sitting beside the stream of water. He raised his cane and went 'bang, bang'. Suddenly, two shots rang out and the beaver fell over dead. What do you think of that?"

The old man said, "I'd say somebody else pumped a couple of rounds into that beaver."

The doctor replied, "My point exactly."

* * * *

A young man was lost wandering in a forest, when he came upon a small house. He knocked on the door and was greeted by an ancient Chinese man with a long, grey beard. "I'm lost," said the man. "Can you put me up for the night?"

"Certainly," the Chinese man said, "but on one condition. If you so much as lay a finger on my daughter, I will inflict upon you the three worst Chinese tortures known to man."

"Okay," said the man, thinking that the daughter must be pretty old as well, and entered the house.

Before dinner, the daughter came down the stairs. She was young, beautiful, and had a fantastic figure. She was obviously attracted to the young man since she couldn't keep her eyes off him during the meal. Remembering the old man's warning, he ignored her and went up to bed alone. But during the night, he could bear it no longer, and sneaked into her room for a night of passion. He was careful to keep everything quiet so the old man wouldn't hear. Near dawn he crept back to his room, exhausted but happy.

He woke to feel a pressure on his chest. Opening his eyes, he saw a large rock on his chest with a note on it that read, "Chinese torture 1: Large rock on chest."

"Well, that's pretty crappy," he thought. "If that's the best the old man can do, then I don't have much to worry about."

He picked the boulder up, walked over to the window and threw the boulder out. As he did so, he noticed another note on it that read: "Chinese torture 2: Rock tied to left testicle."

In a panic, he glanced down and saw the rope that was already getting close to the end. Figuring that a few broken bones was better than castration, he jumped out of the window after the boulder.

As he plummeted, downward he saw a large sign on the ground that read, "Chinese torture 3: Right testicle tied to bedpost."

* * * *

An old Arab lived close to New York City for more than 40 years. He would have loved to plant potatoes in his garden, but he was alone, old and weak. His son was in college in Paris, so the old man sent him an e-mail. He explains the problem:

"Beloved son, I am very sad, because I can't plant potatoes in my garden. I am sure, if only you were here, you would help and dig up the garden for me.

I love you,

Your father"

The following day, the old man received a response e-mail from his son:

"Beloved Father,

Please don't touch the garden. It's there that I have hidden 'the THING'.

I love you, too,

Ahmed"

At 4 p.m., the US Army, The Marines, the FBI, the CIA and the Rangers visited the house of the old man, took the whole garden apart, searched every inch, but couldn't find anything. Disappointed, they leave the house.

A day later, the old man received another e-mail from his son.

"Beloved Father,

I hope the garden is dug up by now and you can plant your potatoes.

That's all I could do for you from here.

I love you,

Ahmed."

* * * *

Q: What's 40 feet long, and smells like piss?

A: A conga line at an old folks home.

* * * *

Old aunts used to come up to me at weddings, poking me in the ribs and cackling, telling me, "You're next." They stopped after I started doing the same thing to them at funerals.

JOKE ANALYSIS
BY DR. BROWN

The Irish die well. This may not be immediately flattering, but it is not an insult. They work for it. Smoking, fighting, eating Irish food, a culturally inoculated form of carrion that is tantamount to an Epikak appetizer and most deadly, spending their lives among other Irish. But most respectable about their departures is their ability to make light of them. Below your will find the last words of Seamus McDonnell, who, at eighty-seven could still spit a full seven-feet while talking. I'll miss him, though he never seemed to miss me.

An elderly Irish gentleman named John Shawnessey is lying on his death bed, awaiting the end. He smells the aroma of chocolate-chip cookies—his favorite.

He decides that, if he must die, he is going to die with the taste of chocolate-chip cookies in his mouth. He slowly and painfully drags himself from his bed. With tremendous effort, he crawls down the stairs and into the kitchen, following the delicious aroma. He enters the kitchen, and spies a plate of chocolate chip cookies on top of the refrigerator.

Summoning the last of his strength, he claws his way up the side of the fridge and takes a cookie. Just as he is about to put it in his mouth, his wife appears and whacks him over the head with a spoon.

"Get away from those cookies, John Shawnessey!" cries his wife. "Those are for the funeral!"

This is an amazing joke! It violates every known tenet of humor, yet still manages to be funny. As an Irish joke, one assumes that the characters will be named Pat or Mike. Here, the lead character goes by "John" and his last name, though undoubtedly of Hiberian extraction misses an "O" that is conspicuous by its absence. Despite the impending wake, alcohol is never mentioned nor is the classic "One less drunk" punchline mentioned. The dying man shows a resolve and tenacity rarely shown by any Celt not addicted to heroin. Moreover, the marital relationship is characterized by only the mildest of violence, and it's displayed by the woman towards the man, completely turning tradition on its head. Despite, or perhaps because of, the complete break from accepted norms of humorous narrative, the joke maintains the readers' suspension of disbelief, even to the point of accepting that an Irish wife would know how to cook anything other than potatoes. It's a magnificent gem, befitting a tale from the emerald isle.

Rest in Peace, Seamus.

FSC 807

ADVANCED FOOD TOXICOLOGY

Course:	FSC 807 Advanced Food Toxicology
Semester:	Fall of even years
Credits:	3
Description:	Toxicology related to food safety. Metabolism of toxicants as influenced by food constituents, mutagenesis, and chemical carcinogenesis. Risk assessment. Your mother's cooking; your cooking and the dangerous crap they serve at that shithole up the block are analyzed. Course may repeat.
Dates:	FALL and SUMMER - Open

"Bite me," "Eat it raw," and "That sucks." Why do we take something a wonderful as eating and go all negative with it? And yet, we also say that an army marches on its stomach, the very route to a man's heart. Feels like a love-hate thing, doesn't it? What it comes down to is this: like working, sleeping and fucking, eating is universal and something most of us could do all day under the right conditions.

—*Steve*

He said, "What have you been doing with all the grocery money I gave you?"

She said, "Turn sideways and look in the mirror."

* * * *

All of his life, Ole had heard stories of an amazing family tradition. It seems that his father, grandfather and great-grandfather had all been able to walk on water on their 21st birthday. On that day, they'd walk across the lake to the boat club for their birthday meal.

So when Ole's 21st birthday came around, he and his pal Sven took a boat out to the middle of the lake. Ole stepped out of the boat and nearly drowned! Sven just managed to pull him to safety.

Furious and confused, Ole went to see his grandmother. "Grandma, it's my 21st birthday, so why can't I walk across the lake like my father, his father, and his father before him?"

Granny looked into Ole's eyes and said, "Because, you dumb nut, your father, grandfather and great-grandfather were born in January. You were born in July."

* * * *

A man asked his wife what she'd like for her birthday. "I'd love to be six again," she replied. On the morning of her birthday, he got her up bright and early, and off they went to a local theme park. What a day! He put her on every ride in the park: the Death Slide, the Screaming Loop, the Wall of Fear — everything there was! Wow! Five hours later she staggered out of the theme park, her head reeling and her stomach upside down. Right to a McDonald's they went, where her husband ordered her a Big Mac along with extra fries and a refreshing chocolate shake.

Then it was off to a movie: the latest Star Wars epic, and hot dogs, popcorn, Pepsi, and M&M's.

What a fabulous adventure! Finally she wobbled home with her husband and collapsed into bed. He leaned over and lovingly asked, "Well, dear, what was it like being six again?"

With one eye open, she said, "You idiot, I meant my dress size!"

* * * *

There was an old Jewish man living in an assisted living center. At 10 PM on a Saturday night, there was a knock on his door. The man opened the door to find a gorgeous 22-year-old blonde wearing nothing but a black see-through negligee. He asked the girl, "What can I do for you?"

The blond looked to him very seductively and said "I am here to offer you super sex."

The man stood there for a minute and looked her up and down and said, "I'll try the soup."

* * * *

"Good evening ladies," Sherlock Holmes said as he passed three women eating bananas on a park bench.

"Do you know them?" Dr. Watson asked.

"No," Holmes replied, "I've never met the nun, the prostitute or the bride we just passed."

"Good Lord, Holmes, how in the world did you know all that?"

"Elementary, my dear Watson. The nun ate the banana by holding it in one hand and using the fingers of the other hand to properly break the fruit into small pieces."

"The prostitute," he continued, "grabbed with both hands and crammed the whole thing into her mouth."

"Amazing!" Watson exclaimed. "But how did you know the third was a newlywed?"

"Because she held it one hand and pushed her head toward it with the other."

* * * *

A guy goes into a restaurant/lounge wearing a shirt open at the collar and is met by a bouncer who tells him he must wear a necktie to gain admission.

So the guy goes out to his car, and he looks around for a necktie and discovers that he just doesn't have one. He sees a set of jumper cables in his trunk. In desperation he ties these around his neck, manages to fashion a fairly acceptable-looking knot and lets the ends dangle free.

He goes back to the restaurant and the bouncer carefully looks him over for a few minutes and then says, "Well, okay, I guess you can come in. Just don't start anything."

* * * *

Two lawyers went into a diner and ordered two drinks. Then they produced sandwiches from their briefcases and started to eat. The waiter became quite concerned and marched over and told them, "You can't eat your own sandwiches in here!"

The attorneys looked at each other, shrugged their shoulders and then exchanged sandwiches.

* * * *

A man goes into a hamburger stand and orders a burger. The waitress takes out two frozen patties and sticks them under her arms. Naturally, the man asked, "What the hell are you doing?!"

The waitress replied, "I'm defrosting them!"

Another guy at the counter pipes up, "In that case, you can cancel my hotdog!"

* * * *

A man observed a sign in the window of a restaurant that read: "Unique Breakfast." So, he walked in and sat down. The waitress brought the man his coffee and asked him what he wanted. "What's your 'Unique Breakfast?'" he asked inquisitively.

"Baked tongue of chicken!" she proudly replied.

"Baked tongue of chicken? Baked tongue of chicken! Do you have any idea how disgusting that is? I would never even consider eating anything that came out of a chicken's mouth!" he fumed.

Undaunted, the waitress asked, "What would you like then?"

"Just bring me some scrambled eggs," the man replied.

* * * *

A waitress walks up to a table with three Japanese men. When she gets to the table, the waitress notices that the three men are furiously masturbating. She asks, "What the hell are you three perverts doing?"

One man replies, "We all very hungry!"

She answers, "But why are you jerking off?"

"Because menu say 'First Come, First Served!'"

* * * *

I once had dinner in a German-Chinese restaurant. The food was delicious, but an hour later, I was hungry for power.

* * * *

A man and woman were having dinner in a fine restaurant. From across the room, their waitress noticed the man begin to slowly slide down in his chair, while the woman remained unconcerned. The waitress watched as the man slid all the way down his chair, and went out of sight under the table and tablecloth. The woman continued to remain calm and unruffled.

The waitress was unable to contain her curiosity. She went over to the table and said to the woman, "Pardon me, ma'am, but I think your husband just slid under the table."

The woman calmly replied, "No, my husband just walked in the door."

* * * *

A man walks into a Chinese restaurant but is told by the maitre'd there will be at least a twenty minute wait and was asked if he'd like to wait in the bar. He goes into the bar and the bartender says, "What'll it be?"

The man replies, "Give me a Stoli with a twist."

The bartender squints at him for a few seconds, then smiles and says, "Once upon time were four little pigs . . ."

* * * *

A blind man walks into a restaurant and sits down.

The waiter, who is also the owner, walks up to the blind man and hands him a menu.

"I'm sorry, sir, but I am blind and can't read the menu. Just bring me a dirty fork from a previous customer, I'll smell it and order from there."

A little confused, the owner walks over to the dirty pile and picks up a greasy fork. He returns to the blind man's table and hands it to him.

The blind man puts the fork to his nose and takes in a deep breath.

"Ah, yes, that's what I'll have, meatloaf and mashed potatoes."

"Unbelievable," the owner says to himself as he walks towards the kitchen.

The cook happens to be the owner's wife and he tells her what had just happened. The blind man eats his meal and leaves.

Several days later the blind man returns and the owner mistakenly brings him a menu again.

"Sir, remember me? I'm the blind man."

"I'm sorry, I didn't recognize you. I'll go get you a dirty fork."

The owner again retrieves a dirty fork and brings it to the blind man.

After another deep breath, the blind man says, "That smells great; I'll take the macaroni and cheese with broccoli."

Once again walking away in disbelief, the owner thinks the blind man is screwing around with him and tells his wife that the next time the blind man comes in he's going to test him.

The blind man eats and leaves.

He returns the following week, but this time the owner sees him coming and runs to the kitchen.

He tells his wife, "Mary, rub this fork on your panties before I take it to the blind man."

Mary complies and hands her husband the fork back.

As the blind man walks in and sits down, the owner is ready and waiting.

"Good afternoon sir, this time I remembered you and I already have the fork ready for you."

The blind man puts the fork to his nose, takes a deep whiff and says, "Hey, I didn't know that Mary worked here?"

* * * *

An Asian guy is having some bread and jam when an American man chuckling and chewing gum, sits down next to him. The Asian ignores the American who, nevertheless, starts a conversation.

American: "You Asian folks eat the whole bread??"

Asian (in a bad mood): "Of course."

American: (after blowing a huge bubble) "We don't. In the States, we only eat what's inside. The crusts we collect in a container, recycle and transform them into croissants and export them to Asia."

The American has a smirk on his face. The Asian listens in silence.

The American persists: "D'ya eat jelly with the bread??"

Asian: "Of course."

American: (cracking his gum between his teeth and chuckling). "We don't. In the States we eat fresh fruit for breakfast, then we put all the peels, seeds, and leftovers in containers, recycle them, transform them into jam and export them to Asia."

The Asian (pissed off) then asks: "Do you have sex in America?"

American: "Why of course we do," the American says with a big smirk.

Asian: And what do you do with the condoms once you've used them?"

American: "We throw them away, of course."

Asian: "We don't. In Asia, we put them in a container, recycle them, melt them down into chewing gum and export them to America."

* * * *

One day, at a New York restaurant, a man suddenly called out, "My son's choking! He swallowed a quarter! Help! Please, anyone! Help!"

A man from a nearby table stood up and announced that he was quite experienced at this sort of thing. He stepped over with almost no look of concern at all, wrapped his hands around the boy's gonads, and squeezed. Out popped the quarter. The man then went back to his table as though nothing had happened.

"Thank you! Thank you!" the father cried. "Are you a paramedic?"

"No," replied the man. "I work for the IRS."

* * * *

A German tourist walks into a McDonald's in New York City and orders a beer. (In Germany and many parts of Europe, McDonald's actually does serve beer.) The local guy in the line behind him immediately gives him the jab: "They don't serve BEER here, you MORON!" The German fellow feels pretty stupid, but suddenly turns to the New Yorker with a surprised look, and begins to chuckle.

"And what's so funny?!?" the New Yorker demands.

"I just realized zat you came here for the food."

* * * *

An Irishman, a Mexican and a blonde guy were doing construction work on scaffolding on the 20th floor of a building.

They were eating lunch and the Irishman said, "Corned beef and cabbage! If I get corned beef and cabbage one more time for lunch, I'm going to jump off this building."

The Mexican opened his lunch box and exclaimed, "Burritos again! If I get burritos one more time, I'm going to jump off, too."

The blond opened his lunch and said, "Bologna again! If I get a bologna sandwich one more time, I'm jumping too."

The next day, the Irishman opened his lunch box, saw corned beef and cabbage, and jumped to his death. The Mexican opened his lunch, saw a burrito, and jumped, too. The blonde guy opened his lunch, saw the bologna and jumped to his death as well.

At the funeral, the Irishman's wife was weeping. She said, "If I'd known how really tired he was of corned beef and cabbage, I never would have given it to him again!" The Mexican's wife also wept and said, "I could have given him tacos or enchiladas! I didn't realize he hated burritos so much." Everyone turned and stared at the blonde's wife. The blonde's wife said, "Don't look at me. He makes his own lunch."

* * * *

Gary and Mary go on their honeymoon, and Gary spends six hours of the honeymoon performing oral sex on Mary. The next afternoon, they go to an Italian restaurant. Suddenly, Gary starts to freak out. He screams, "Waiter! Waiter! Come over here!"

The waiter says, "Can I help you, sir?" Gary yells, "There's a hair in my spaghetti! Get it out of here!" The waiter apologizes up and down as he quickly takes the spaghetti away.

Mary looks over at Gary, and shaking her head, she whispers, "What a hypocrite you are. You spent most of last night with your face full of hair."

Gary says, "Yeah? Well, how long do you think I'd have stayed if I found a piece of spaghetti in there?"

* * * *

A man goes to a restaurant, orders some takeout, and sits down to wait for his food. While he waits, he grabs a handful of peanuts from the bowl on the counter, and as he starts to chew, he hears a voice say, "That's a beautiful tie. Is that silk? Very NICE choice!"

Wondering who made the comment, he looks around and doesn't see anyone nearby who could be speaking to him. With a shrug, he pops a few more peanuts into his mouth.

Next he hears the voice say, "Those shoes are stylin', my man. Are they Italian leather? They look GRRREAT!"

He whirls around again, but sees no one near him. He glances nervously around and then at his shoes, which he tucks self-consciously under the stool.

A little freaked out, he grabs another handful of peanuts. This time the voice continues with, "That suit looks FANTASTIC! Is it an Armani? Very nice!"

He immediately calls the waiter over and says, "Look. I keep hearing these voices telling me how great my tie, my shoes, and my suit look - what's up with that? Am I GOING CRAZY??"

"Oh," the waiter nonchalantly replies. "It's just the peanuts."

"The PEANUTS?!?" the astonished man asks, staring at the bowl beside him.

"Yes," replies the waiter, "they're complimentary."

****

Early one morning the Mole family awoke, and Daddy mole climbed to the top of the mole hole and sniffed the air.

"I smell bacon frying," he said.

Momma mole crowded in beside him and sniffed the air, "I smell eggs cooking," she said.

Baby mole tried and tried to get to the top but there was no room left so he said, "All I can smell is molasses!"

****

It was mealtime during a flight on a small airline in the northwest. "Would you like dinner?" the flight attendant asked the man seated in front of me.

"What are my choices?" he asked.

"Yes or no," she replied.

****

A man walks into a greasy spoon diner, sits up at the counter and orders a hamburger. The cook reaches into a container of ground beef with his bare hand and pulls out a wad of beef. He slaps the wad into his bare armpit and flattens it by flapping his arms.

The man turns to the patron on his right and says, "Oh my God! That's the grossest thing I've ever seen!"

The other customer replies, "Oh hell, that's nothing. You should come here in the morning when he is making donuts!"

* * * *

The day after a man lost his wife in a scuba diving accident, he was greeted by two grim-faced policemen at his door.

"We're sorry to call on you at this hour, Mr. Wilkens, but we have some information about your wife."

"Well, tell me!" the man said.

The policeman said, "We have some bad news, some good news and some really great news. Which do you want to hear first?"

Fearing the worse, Mr. Wilkens said, "Give me the bad news first."

So the policeman said, "I'm sorry to tell you sir, but this morning we found your wife's body in San Francisco Bay."

"Oh my god!," said Mr. Wilkens, overcome by emotion. Then, remembering what the policeman had said, he asked, "What's the good news?"

"Well," said the policeman, "When we pulled her up she had two five-pound lobsters and a dozen good size Dungeoness crabs on her."

"If that's the good news than what's the great news?!" Mr. Wilkens demanded.

The policeman said, "We're going to pull her up again tomorrow morning."

* * * *

A guy kills a deer, brings it to the house and cooks it for dinner, but does not tell his frat bothers what it is. He told them he would give them a clue.

"It's what my girlfriend calls me sometimes."

Almost immediately, one of the brothers yells, "Don't eat it! It's a fucking asshole!"

* * * *

A businessman had arranged an important formal dinner party at his home where they were going to serve stuffed whole baked fish as the main course. While the guests were eating the appetizer, the cook came to the host and whispered "Please come urgently to the kitchen." The host went to the kitchen where the cook explained that while she was serving the starter, the cat ate a big chunk of the fish which they were going to serve. The host said, "Just fill the hole with stuffing and turn the other side up. Nobody will notice."

The fish was served and when they were nearly finished eating, the host was again called to the kitchen. The cook said, "The cat is dead!"

The host rushed back to the dinner party and apologized, "Something was wrong with the fish and everyone must have their stomachs pumped out at the hospital!"

When he came back from the hospital, and the host went to ask the cook, "Where is the cat?"

"Oh," said the chef, "the cat is still by the road where the truck ran it down!"

* * * *

Question: Why do vegetarian women not make a sound when they orgasm during sex?

Answer: Because they don't want to admit that a piece of meat can give them so much pleasure!

* * * *

Q: How do you get a drummer off your porch?
A: Pay him for the pizza.

* * * *

Bill worked in a pickle factory. He had been employed there for a number of years when he came home one day to confess to his wife that he had a terrible compulsion. He had an urge to stick his penis into the pickle slicer. His wife suggested that he should see a sex therapist to talk about it, but Bill indicated that he'd be too embarrassed. He vowed to overcome the compulsion on his own. One day a few weeks later, Bill came home absolutely ashen. His wife could see at once that something was seriously wrong. "What's wrong, Bill?" she asked.

"Do you remember that I told you how I had this tremendous urge to put my penis into the pickle slicer?"

"Oh, Bill, you didn't."

"Yes, I did."

"My God, Bill, what happened?"

"I got fired."

"No, Bill. I mean, what happened with the pickle slicer?"

"Oh...she got fired too."

* * * *

A man gets up one morning to find his wife already in the kitchen cooking. He looks to see what she's cooking, and sees one of his socks in the frying pan. "What are you doing?" he asks.

"I'm doing what you asked me to do last night when you came to bed very drunk, " she replied.

Completely puzzled, the man walks away thinking to himself, "I don't remember asking her to . . . cook my sock . . ."

* * * *

A guy married this woman. Unfortunately, his dick was too small, so every time they had sex, he used a pickle instead of his dick. For seven years he has been doing that. One night his wife suspect that something is wrong so while they are having sex she quickly threw back the covers and turned on the lights.

So the woman said, "What the hell is that, are you using a pickle on me? I am shocked, and for seven years you have been doing that, you piece of shit!"

So the man said, "Shut up! It's been seven years and I never asked where the hell those kids came from!"

* * * *

A man and a woman are riding next to each other in first class. The man sneezes, pulls out his wang and wipes the tip off. The woman can't believe what she just saw and decides she is hallucinating. A few minutes pass. The man sneezes again. He pulls out his wang and wipes the tip off. The woman is about to go nuts. She can't believe that such a rude person exists. A few minutes pass. The man sneezes yet again. He takes his wang out and wipes the tip off. The woman has finally had enough. She turns to the man and says, "Three times you've sneezed, and three times you've removed your penis from your pants to wipe it off! What the hell kind of degenerate are you?"

The man replies, "I'm sorry to have disturbed you, ma'am. I have a very rare condition such that when I sneeze, I have an orgasm."

The woman then says, "Oh, how strange. What are you taking for it?"

"Pepper."

* * * *

A man is dining in a fancy restaurant and there is a gorgeous redhead sitting at the next table. He has been checking her out since he sat down, but lacks the nerve to start a conversation. Suddenly she sneezes, and her glass eye comes flying out of its socket towards the man.

He reflexively reaches out, grabs it out of the air, and hands it back.

"Oh my, I am so sorry," the woman says as he pops her eye back in place. "Let me buy your dinner to make it up to you," she says.

They enjoy a wonderful dinner together, and afterwards they go to the theater followed by drinks. They talk, they laugh, she shares her deepest dreams and he shares his. She listens. After paying for everything, she asks him if he would like to come to her place for a nightcap . . . and stay for breakfast.

They have a wonderful, wonderful time.

The next morning, she cooks a gourmet meal with all the trimmings. The guy is amazed! Everything has been so incredible! "You know," he said, "you are the perfect woman. Are you this nice to every guy you meet?"

"No," she replies, "You just happened to catch my eye."

* * * *

A woman is very distressed because she has not been married very long, and yet her husband has lost interest in having sex. So, she goes to see her doctor, and relays the problem. The doctor doesn't seem worried at all and tells her that this is nothing serious, that her husband has merely lost his animal instincts. The doctor tells her to crumble some dog biscuits on her husband's cereal every morning without telling him, and little by little this will bring out the savage beast in him. He wishes her good luck and tells her to come back in a week with a progress report.

A week later the woman returns to the doctor, who asks how her husband is. "He's dead," she replies.

"Dead?" the doctor asked. "What happened?"

The woman replied, "He was sitting on the driveway licking himself, and I backed over him with the car."

* * * *

A beautiful woman loved growing tomatoes, but couldn't seem to get her tomatoes to turn red. One day while taking a stroll, she came upon a gentlemen neighbor who had the most beautiful garden full of huge red tomatoes. The woman asked the gentlemen, "What do you do to get your tomatoes red?"

The gentlemen responded, "Well, twice a day I stand in front of my tomato garden and expose myself, and my tomatoes turn red from blushing so much." The woman was so impressed; she decided to try doing the same thing to her tomato garden to see if it would work. So twice a day for two weeks she exposed herself to her garden hoping for the best. One day the gentlemen was passing by and asked the woman, "By the way, how did you make out? Did your tomatoes turn red?"

"No," she replied, "but my cucumbers are enormous."

* * * *

A timeless lesson on how consultants can make a difference for an organization. Last week, we took some friends out to a new restaurant, and noticed that the waiter who took our order carried a spoon in his shirt pocket. It seemed a little strange. When the busboy brought our water and utensils, I noticed he also had a spoon in his shirt pocket. Then I looked around saw that all the staff had spoons in their pockets.

When the waiter came back to serve our soup I asked, "Why the spoon?"

"Well," he explained, "The restaurant's owners hired Andersen Consulting to revamp all our processes. After several months of analysis, they concluded that the spoon was the most frequently dropped utensil. It represents a drop frequency of approximately three spoons per table per hour. If our personnel are better prepared, we can reduce the number of trips back to the kitchen and save 15 man-hours per shift." As luck would have it, I dropped my spoon and he was able to replace it with his spare. "I'll get another spoon next time I go to the kitchen instead of making an extra trip to get it right now."

I was impressed. I also noticed that there was a string hanging out of the waiter's fly. Looking around, I noticed that all the waiters had the same string hanging from their flies. So before he walked off, I asked the waiter, "Excuse me, but can you tell me why you have that string right there?"

"Oh, certainly!" Then he lowered his voice. "Not everyone is so observant. That consulting firm I mentioned also found out that we could save time in the restroom. By tying this string to the tip of you know what, we can pull it out without touching it and eliminate the need to wash our hands, shortening the time spent in the restroom by 76.39 percent."

I asked, "After you get it out, how do you put it back?"

"Well, " he whispered, "I don't know about the others, but I use the spoon."

* * * *

A cop is patrolling Lover's Lane when he sees the strangest thing. A young teenage couple is sitting in a car, the guy in the front and the girl in the back. The guy is munching on an apple and reading a magazine and the girl appears to be sucking on a lollipop and knitting. He stops the patrol car and walks over to knock on the young man's window. He rolls the window down.

"Yes officer?"

"I have to ask you, what are you doing?"

"Well sir, I am reading a magazine."

"What about the young lady in the backseat?"

The young man turns to look behind him. "Well, I think she is knitting a pullover sweater."

"How old are you young man?" the officer asks.

"I am twenty-five, Officer."

"And the girl?' The young man looks at his watch. "Well, she'll be 18 in 11 minutes."

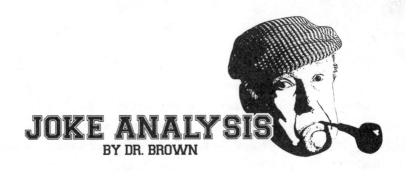

JOKE ANALYSIS
BY DR. BROWN

To a cannibal, the term "playing with your food" means promising to set a prisoner free if they do the chicken dance, but once they have, eating them anyway. Food plays an integral role in the fabric of life, giving flight to humor from myriad perspectives: jokes over meals, jokes about meals and, for the very poor, jokes as meals.

The following joke was overheard in a cafeteria when told by one pampered young co-ed to another before she was summoned away by a well-healed lacrosse player several credits her senior.

A husband and wife were having a fine dining experience at their exclusive country club when this stunning young woman comes over to their table, gives the husband a big kiss, says she'll see him later and walks away.

His wife glares at him and says, "Who was that?!"

"Oh," replies the husband, "she's my mistress."

"Well that's the last straw," says the wife. "I've had enough, I want a divorce. I am going to hire the most aggressive, meanest divorce lawyer I can find and make your life miserable."

"I can understand that," replies her husband, "but remember, if we get a divorce, it will mean no more wintering in Key West, or the Caribbean, no more summers in Tuscany, no more Cadillacs in the garage, and no more country club, and we'll have to sell the 26-room house and move to two smaller homes, but the decision is yours."

Just then, a mutual friend enters the restaurant with a gorgeous young woman on his arm.

"Who's that with Jim?" asks the wife.

"That's his mistress," says her husband.

The wife replies, "Ours is prettier."

While this joke seems, at first glance, to be perfectly crafted, it is in fact seriously flawed.

If the husband and wife are members of an exclusive country club, then it goes without saying that they are WASPs. A country club that allows a Jew or an African-American into its ranks will soon enough allow an Irishman in, out of some misplaced feeling of civic duty. And should an Irishman be allowed into a club, soon his hundreds of brothers and cousins will invite themselves over for drinks, rendering the bar area impassable. Nor will it be possible to get them to leave.

No, no. Exclusive country clubs, by definition, exclude.

Yet the idea that a WASP husband and wife could eat a meal together in anything other than a stony silence stretches credulity to the breaking point.

Moreover, if the protagonists are indeed Anglo-Saxons, then it is virtually impossible to believe that the husband would have a beautiful mistress.

By the age of thirty, most Anglo-Saxon men are incapable of feeling normal heterosexual desire. Most libidinal instincts have been suppressed by years of saltpeter at boarding school, and those sexual feelings that remain are nearly always either highly fetishized longings for scat play and pony-boy training, or overwhelming yearnings for anonymous transvestite buggery in dark city side streets.

Thus while the phrase "mistress" is correct in the anecdote, to be perfectly accurate, the wife should reply, "Ours looks stricter."

Or, alternatively, "At least ours is passable."

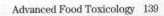

TRAN 414
GEOGRAPHY OF
TRANSPORTATION

Course:	GEO 414 Geography of Transportation
Semester:	Fall of odd years
Credits:	3
Prerequisite:	GEO 113
Restrictions:	Not open to freshmen.
Description:	Spatial principles of transportation. Theories of interaction, network structures, and location-allocation models. "Segways," "Vespas" and "Mopeds" will be fascinating in the first session, then completely forgotten. Classes may be delayed due to construction work on hallways.
Dates:	SUMMER - Open

Have you ever been blown while driving a car? Are you a member of the mile high club? How about the sleeper cabin of a train or ship; ever done it there? For every means of travel, there is a way to have sex (though the bicycle could require some circus skills). This remarkable fact has little to do with the content of the following jokes, other than the travel part, but it does make you think, doesn't it?

—*Steve*

A trucker who was driving his fully-loaded rig up a steep hill and was starting down the equally steep other side noticed a man and woman lying in the middle of the road, making love. He blew the air horn several times as he was bearing down on them. Realizing they were not about to get out of the way, he slammed on his brakes and stopped just inches from them. Getting out of the cab, madder than hell, the trucker looked down at the two, still in the middle of the road and yelled, "What the hell is the matter with you two? Didn't you hear me blowing the horn? You could've been killed!"

The man on the road, obviously satisfied and not too concerned, looked up and said, "Look I was coming, she was coming, you were coming. You were the only one with brakes."

* * * *

A successful businessman flew to Vegas for the weekend to gamble. He lost the shirt off his back, and had nothing left but a quarter and the second half of his round-trip ticket. If he could just get to the airport, he could get himself home. So he went out to the front of the casino where there was a cab waiting. He got in and explained his situation to the cabbie. He promised to send the driver money from home. He offered him his credit card numbers, his drivers license number and his address, but it was to no avail.

The cabbie said, "If you don't have fifteen dollars, get the hell out of my cab!" So the businessman was forced to hitch-hike to the airport, and was barely in time to catch his flight.

One year later, the businessman, having worked long and hard to regain his financial success, returned to Vegas and this time he won big. Feeling pretty good about himself, he went out to the front of the casino to get a cab ride back to the airport.

Well, who should he see out there, at the end of a long line of cabs? His old buddy who had refused to give him a ride when he was down on his luck.

The businessman thought for a moment about how he could make the guy pay for his lack of charity, and he hit on a plan. The businessman got in the first cab in the line, "How much for a ride to the airport?" he asked.

"Fifteen bucks," came the reply. "And how much for you to give me a blowjob on the way?"

"What?! Get the hell out of my cab."

The businessman got into the back of each cab in the long line and asked the same questions, with the same result. When he got to his old friend at the back of the line, he got in and asked "How much for a ride to the airport?"

The cabbie replied, "Fifteen bucks."

The businessman said, "Okay." And off they went.

Then, as they drove slowly past the long line of cabs, the businessman gave a big smile and thumbs up sign to each driver.

* * * *

A man boarded an airplane and took his seat. As he settled in, he glanced up and saw the most beautiful woman boarding the plane. He soon realized that she was heading straight towards his seat.

As fate would have it, she took the seat right beside his. Eager to strike up a conversation, he blurted out, "Business trip or pleasure?"

She turned, smiled and said, "Business. I'm going to the annual Nymphomaniacs of America Convention in Chicago."

He swallowed hard.

Here was the most gorgeous woman he had ever seen sitting next to him, and she was going to a meeting for nymphomaniacs! Struggling to maintain his composure, he calmly asked, "What's your business role at the convention?"

"Lecture," she responded. "I am the lead lecturer where I use information that I have learned from my own personal experiences to debunk some of the popular myths about sexuality."

"Really," he said, "and what kinds of myths are there?"

"Well," she explained, "one popular myth is that African-American men are the most well-endowed of all men, when in fact it is the Native American Indian who is most likely to possess that trait. Another popular myth is that Frenchmen are the best lovers, when actually it is the men of Jewish descent who are the best. I have also discovered that the lover with the absolutely best stamina is the Southern Redneck . . ."

Suddenly the woman became a little uncomfortable and blushed. "I'm sorry," she said, "I shouldn't really be discussing all this with you. I don't even know your name."

"Tonto", the man said, "Tonto Goldstein. But my friends call me Bubba."

* * * *

A police officer pulls a guy over for speeding and has the following exchange:

Officer: May I see your driver's license?

Driver: I don't have one. It was revoked when I got my fifth DWI.

Officer: May I see the registration for this vehicle?

Driver: It's not my car. I stole it.

Officer: The car is stolen?

Driver: That's right. But come to think of it, I think I saw the registration in the glove box when I was putting my gun in there.

Officer: There's a gun in the glove box?

Driver: Yes sir. That's where I put it after I shot and killed the woman who owns this car and stuffed her in the trunk.

Officer: There's a BODY in the TRUNK?!?!?

Driver: Yes, sir.

Hearing this, the officer immediately called his Captain. The car was quickly surrounded by police, and the Captain approached the driver to handle the tense situation:

Captain: Sir, can I see your license?

Driver: Sure. Here it is.

It was valid.

Captain: Whose car is this?

Driver: It's mine, officer. Here's the registration.

The driver owned the car.

Captain: Could you slowly open your glove box so I can see if there's a gun in it?

Driver: Yes, sir, but there's no gun in it.

Sure enough, there was nothing in the glove box.

Captain: Would you mind opening your trunk? I was told you said there's a body in it.

Driver: No problem.

Trunk is opened; no body.

Captain: I don't understand it. The officer who stopped you said you told him you didn't have a license, stole the car, had a gun in the glovebox, and that there was a dead body in the trunk.

Driver: I'll bet he told you I was speeding, too!

* * * *

A blonde and a lawyer are seated next to each other on a flight from Los Angeles to New York. The lawyer asks if she would like to play a fun game.

The blonde, tired, just wants to take a nap, politely declines and rolls over to the window to catch a few winks. The lawyer persists and explains that the game is easy and a lot of fun. He explains, "I ask you a question, and if you don't know the answer, you pay me $5, and vise versa."

Again, she declines and tries to get some sleep. The lawyer, now agitated, says, "Okay, if you don't know the answer you pay me $5, and if I don't know the answer, I will pay you $500."

This catches the blonde's attention and, figuring there will be no end to this torment unless she plays, agrees to the game.

The lawyer asks the first question. "What's the distance from the earth to the moon?"

The blonde doesn't say a word, reaches into her purse, pulls out a $5 bill and hands it to the lawyer.

"Okay," says the lawyer, "your turn."

She asks the lawyer, "What goes up a hill with three legs and comes down with four legs?"

The lawyer, puzzled, takes out his laptop computer and searches all his references, no answer. He taps into the air phone with his modem and searches the net and the Library of Congress, no answer. Frustrated, he sends e-mails to all his friends and coworkers, to no avail. After an hour, he wakes the blonde, and hands her $500.

The blonde says, "Thank you," and turns back to get some more sleep.

The lawyer, who is more than a little miffed, wakes the blonde and asks, "Well, what's the answer?"

Without a word, the blonde reaches into her purse, hands the lawyer $5, and goes back to sleep. And you thought blondes were dumb.

* * * *

A young single guy is on a cruise ship, having the time of his life. On the second day of the cruise, the ship slams into an iceberg and begins to sink. Passengers around him are screaming, flailing, and drowning but our guy manages to grab on to a piece of driftwood, and using every last ounce of strength, swims a few miles through the shark-infested sea to a remote island.

Sprawled on the shore nearly passed out from exhaustion, he turns his head and sees a woman lying near him, unconscious, barely breathing. She's also managed to wash up on shore from the sinking ship.

He makes his way to her, and with some mouth-to-mouth assistance, he manages to get her breathing again. She looks up at him, wide-eyed and grateful and says, "My God, you saved my life!" He suddenly realizes the woman is Jessica Alba!

Days and weeks go by. Jessica and our guy are living on the island together. They've set up a hut, there's fruit on the trees, and they're in heaven. Jessica's fallen madly in love with our man, and they're making passionate love morning, noon and night.

Alas, one day she notices he's looking kind of glum. "What's the matter, sweetheart?" she asks. "We have a wonderful life together. I'm in love with you. Is there something wrong? Is there anything I can do?"

He says, "Actually, Jessica, there is. Would you mind, putting on my shirt?"

"Sure," she says, "if it will help." He takes off his shirt and she puts it on.

"Now would you put on my pants?" he asks.

"Sure, honey, if it's really going to make you feel better," she says.

"Okay, would you put on my hat now, and draw a little mustache on your face?" he asks.

"Whatever you want, sweetie," she says, and does.

Then he says, "Now, would you start walking around the edge of the island?"

She starts walking around the perimeter of the island. He sets off in the other direction. They meet up half way around the island a few minutes later. He rushes up to her, grabs her by the shoulders, and says, "Dude! You'll never believe who I'm fucking!"

* * * *

A man came home from work sporting two black eyes. "What happened to you?" asked his wife.

"I'll never understand women," he replied. "I was riding up in an escalator behind this pretty young girl, and I noticed that her skirt was stuck in the crack of her ass. So I pulled it out, and she turned around and punched me in the eye!"

"I can certainly appreciate that," said the wife. "But how did you get the second black eye?"

"Well, I figured she liked it that way," said the husband. "So I pushed it back in."

* * * *

Mrs. Davis has three daughters who are all getting married within the same month. She tells each one of her daughters to write back about their married life. To avoid possible embarrassment to their new husbands by openly discussing their love lives, the mother and daughters agree to use newspaper advertisements as a "code" to let the mother know how their love lives are going. The first one gets married and the second day a telegram arrives with a single message, simply: "MAXWELL HOUSE COFFEE."

Mrs. Davis gets the newspaper and checks the Maxwell House Coffee advertisement, and it says: "Good to the last drop . . ." So, Mrs. Davis is happy.

Then the second daughter gets married. After a week, there is a postcard that reads: "ROTHMAN'S MATTRESSES." So, Mrs. Davis looks at the Rothman's Mattresses ad, and it says: "FULL SIZE, KING SIZE." And Mrs. Davis is happy.

Then it is the third one's wedding. Mrs. Davis is anxious because two weeks have passed and still no message from the third daughter. Then after four weeks comes a letter with the message: "BRITISH AIRWAYS."

And Mrs. Davis looks into the British Airways ad, but this time she faints. The ad reads: "THREE TIMES A DAY, SEVEN DAYS A WEEK, BOTH WAYS."

* * * *

An 85-year old husband and wife decide to take a road trip. She drives because she can see, and he rides because he can hear.

After traveling for a while, they get pulled over by a State Trooper.

She rolls down her window and the cop says "I need to see your drivers license and vehicle registration, please."

The woman turns to her husband and shouts "WHAT DID HE SAY?"

The husband replies, "HE WANTS YOUR LICENSE AND REGISTRATION!"

The woman gives the documents to the officer and after studying her license the cop says, "Oh, you're from Chicago. I've been there. Actually, the worst piece of ass I ever had was in Chicago!"

The woman turns to her husband and shouts "WHAT DID HE SAY?"

And the husband replies, "HE SAYS HE KNOWS YOU!"

* * * *

A woman phones up her boyfriend at work for a chat . . .

Says He: "I'm sorry honey, but I'm up to my neck in work today"

Says She: "But I've got some good news and some bad news for you dear."

Says He: "OK darling, but since I've got no time now, just give me the good news."

Says She: "Well, the air bag works . . ."

* * * *

On Christmas morning, a cop on horseback is sitting at a traffic light, and next to him is a kid on his shiny new bike. The cop says to the kid, "Nice bike you got there. Did Santa bring that to you?"

The kid replies, "Yeah."

The cop says, "Well, next year tell Santa to put a tail-light on that bike." The cop then proceeds to issue the kid a ticket for the bicycle safety violation.

The kid takes the ticket and before he rides off, he turns back and noticing the horse is a mare, says to the cop, "By the way, that's a nice horse you got there. Did Santa bring that to you?"

Humoring the kid, the cop says, "Yeah, he sure did."

The kid says, "Well, next year tell Santa to put the dick under the horse rather than on top."

＊＊＊＊

A blonde decides try horse back riding unassisted without prior experience or lessons. She mounts the horse with great effort, and the tall, shiny horse springs into motion.

It gallops along at a steady and rhythmic pace, but the blonde begins to slip from the saddle. Out of sheer terror, she grabs for the horse's mane, but cannot seem to get a firm grip. She tries to throw her arms around the horse's neck, but she slides down the side of the horse anyway. The horse gallops along, seemingly oblivious to its slipping rider.

Finally, giving up her frail grip, she leaps away from the horse to try and throw herself to safety.

Unfortunately, her foot has become entangled in the stirrup. She is now at the mercy of the horse's pounding hooves as her head is struck against the ground again and again. As her head is battered against the ground, she is mere moments away from unconsciousness or even death when Frank, the Wal-Mart manager runs out and unplugs the horse.

＊＊＊＊

A very successful lawyer parked his brand new Lexus in front of his office ready to show it off to his colleagues. As he got out, a truck came along too close to the curb and completely tore off the driver's door.

Fortunately, a cop in a police car was close enough to see the accident and pulled up behind the Lexus with his lights flashing. Before the cop had a chance to ask any questions, the lawyer started screaming hysterically about how his Lexus which he had just picked up the day before was now completely ruined and would never be the same no matter how the body shop tried to make it whole again.

After the lawyer finally wound down from his rant, the cop shook his head in disgust and disbelief. "I can't believe how materialistic you lawyers are," he said. "You are so focused on your possessions that you neglect the most important things in life."

"How can you say such a thing?" said the lawyer.

The cop replied, "Don't you even realize that your left arm is missing? It got ripped off when the truck hit you!"

"Oh, my God!" screamed the lawyer. "MY ROLEX!"

* * * *

A motorcycle cop had just pulled over a red Porsche after it had run a stop sign.

"May I see your driver's license and registration please?"

"What's the problem, officer?"

"You just ran that stop sign back there."

"Oh come on, pal, there wasn't a car within miles of me."

"Nevertheless, sir, you are required to come to complete stop, look both ways, and proceed with caution."

"You gotta be kidding me."

"It's no joke, sir."

"Look, I slowed down almost to a complete stop, saw no one within twenty miles, and proceeded with caution."

"That's beside the point, sir. You are supposed to come to a complete stop, and you didn't. Now, if I may see your license and . . ."

"You've got a lot of time on your hands, pal. What's the matter, all the donut shops closed?"

"Sir, I'll overlook that last comment. Your license and registration, please."

"I will, if you can tell me the difference between slowing down and coming to a complete stop."

The policeman had enough.

"Sir, I can do better than that."

He opened the car door, dragged the rude motorist out, and proceeded to methodically beat him over the head with his nightstick.

"Now, sir, would you like for me to slow down or come to complete stop?"

* * * *

The Pope has just finished a tour of Napa Valley and is taking a limousine to San Francisco. Having never driven a limo, the Pope asks the chauffeur if he might drive for a while. Well, the chauffeur doesn't have much choice, so he climbs in the back of the limo and the Pope takes the wheel.

The Pope proceeds down Silverado, and starts accelerating to see what the limo can do. He gets to about 90 mph, and suddenly he sees the red and blue lights of a CHP cruiser in his mirror. He pulls over and the trooper comes to his window. The trooper, seeing who it is, says, "Just a moment please, I need to call in."

The trooper calls in and asks for the chief. He tells the chief that he's got a REALLY important person pulled over, and asks how to handle it.

"It's not Ted Kennedy again, is it?" asks the chief.

"No, Sir!" replies the trooper. "This guy's more important."

"Is it the governor?"

"No! Even more important!"

"Is it the PRESIDENT?"

"No! Even more important!"

"Well, WHO THE HECK is it?" screams the chief.

"I don't know, Sir," replies the trooper, "But he's got the Pope as his chauffeur!

* * * *

A blonde's house is on fire so she runs outside to use a payphone to call for help. She gets the 911 operator, and gets transferred to the firehouse.

"Mr. Fireman, my house is on fire you have to help me!"

The Fireman replies, "Yes, yes, Miss, how do I get to your house?"

The blonde pauses a moment, and replies, "Umm, it's the house that's on fire." Realizing he is now talking to a blonde, the fireman comes back with, "No, Miss, how would you like me to get to your house?"

To which the blonde replies, "Duh, big red truck."

* * * *

Police are called to a pedestrian struck by a train. The pedestrian's body parts are strewn along the tracks for about a mile. The officers started to collect the parts in order to identify the deceased. Eventually the head was found in a ditch beside the rails. A policeman picks it up and walks into a local bar not far from the tracks. As he walks into the bar he holds the head up high for all to see and says, "Does anyone recognize this guy?"

All the patrons turn on their stools and have a look. One of them pipes up and says "Well, he kinda looks like my brother, 'cept my brother's not that tall."

* * * *

One dark night outside a small town, a fire started inside the local chemical plant. Before long, it exploded into flames and an alarm went out to fire departments from miles around. After fighting the fire for over an hour, the chemical company president approached the fire chief and said, "All of our secret formulas are in the vault in the center of the plant. They must be saved! I will give $50,000 to the engine crew that brings them out safely!"

As soon as the chief heard this, he ordered the firemen to strengthen their attack on the blaze. After two more hours of attacking the fire, president of the company offered $100,000 to the engine company that could bring out the company's secret files.

From the distance, a long siren was heard and another fire truck came into sight. It was a local volunteer fire department composed entirely of men over 65. To everyone's amazement, the little fire engine raced through the chemical plant gates and drove straight into the middle of the inferno.

In the distance, the other firemen watched as the old-timers hopped off of their rig and began to fight the fire with an effort that they had never seen before. After an hour of intense fighting, the volunteer company had extinguished the fire and saved the secret formulas.

Joyous, the chemical company president announced that he would double the reward to $200,000 and walked over to personally thank each of the volunteers. After thanking each of the old men individually, the president asked the group what they intended to do with the reward money.

The fire truck driver looked him right in the eye and said, "The first thing we're going to do is fix the dang brakes on that truck!"

* * * *

A little old Amish lady is trotting down the road in her horse and buggy when she is pulled over by a cop.

"Ma'am, I'm not going to ticket you, but I do have to issue you a warning. You have a broken reflector on your buggy."

"Oh, I'll let my husband Jacob know as soon as I get home," said the little old Amish lady.

"That's fine," said the officer.

"Another thing, ma'am. I don't like the way that one rein loops across the horse's back and around one of his testicles. I consider that animal abuse. That's cruelty to animals. Have your husband take care of that right away!"

Later that day, the little old Amish lady is home telling her husband about her encounter with the cop.

"Well, what exactly did he say?" said the husband.

"He said the reflector is broken."

"I can fix that in two minutes. What else?"

"I'm not sure," she said, "something about the emergency brake . . ."

* * * *

A couple drove down a country road for several miles, not saying a word. An earlier discussion had led to an argument and neither of them wanted to concede their position. As they passed a barnyard of mules, jackasses, and pigs, the husband replied sarcastically, "Relatives of yours?"

"Yep," the wife replied, "in-laws."

* * * *

A bus stops and two Italian men get on. They sit down and engage in an animated conversation. The lady sitting behind them ignores them at first, but her attention is galvanized when she hears one of the men say the following:

"Emma come first. Den I come. Den two asses come together. I come once-a-more. Two asses, they come together again. I come again and pee twice. Then I come one lasta time."

"You foul-mouthed sex-obsessed swine," retorted the lady indignantly. "In this country . . . we don't speak aloud in public places about our sex lives."

"Hey, coola down lady," said the man. "Who talkin' abouta sexa? I'm a justa tellin' my frienda how to spella 'Mississippi'."

* * * *

A preacher and an unsafe cab driver both died the same day and went to Heaven.

When they arrived at the gate, St. Peter greeted them. The cab driver got there first, so Peter gave him his beautiful, shiny robe and a beautiful set of wings to go with it.

"Wow," the preacher thought to himself. "If he got all that just being a cab driver, then think of how beautiful my robe and wings will be since I am a preacher!"

Peter called the preacher up front to get his robe and wings. His robe was a simple cotton robe and his wings were sort of small compared to the cab driver's wings.

Bewildered, the preacher decided to ask Peter what happened. So he went back to Peter and asked him, "Why did the cab driver get such a beautiful robe and wings and I, a preacher, get simple cotton?"

Peter smiled and replied, "When you preached, people went to sleep. When he drove they prayed."

* * * *

A mother and her son were flying Southwest Airlines from Kansas City to Chicago.

The son (who had been looking out the window) turned to his mother and asked,

"If big dogs have baby dogs, and big cats have baby cats, why don't big planes have baby planes?"

The mother (who couldn't think of an answer) told her son to ask the stewardess.

So the boy asked the stewardess, "If big dogs have baby dogs, and big cats have baby cats, why don't big planes have baby planes?"

The stewardess responded, "Did your mother tell you to ask me?"

The boy said, "Yes, she did."

"Well, then, tell your mother that there are no baby planes because Southwest always pulls out on time."

JOKE ANALYSIS
BY DR. BROWN

Advancing age manifests itself it various ways. Two of the most prominent are a loss in driving skills, the onset of which is always indicated with a desire to continuously signal left, and one's first name. There are precious few old people named Jason, Tiffany, Tamaqua or Dylan. Therefore, if the protagonist of a joke is named Irving, and the scenario is placed in Florida, you know you have a relic on your hands.

Our joke was imparted to me by an elder statesman named Aidan, the current most popular boy's name, making him the exception that makes the rule.

This old guy is driving down I-95 in Florida returning to Century Village and his wife calls on the cell phone, "Irving," she says, "Be careful! On the news, they said there is a maniac going the wrong way down the highway!"

Irving replies, "No, Goldie, there are hundreds of them!"

This entry begs the question: would the joke be funnier, if there were a Chinaman at the wheel? Authorities differ.

Some argue that the tragi-comic nature is heightened because of the universality of the aging process. We can all relate to the very real problems of advancing senile dementia.

Other experts stand that same point on its head, noting that it is far less fun to laugh at yourself than it is to laugh at somebody else. Therefore, assuming you aren't Chinese, the joke is much funnier when told in a thick Mandarin accent. For further hilarity, instead of "hundreds" of cars going the wrong way, substitute the phrase "rots of them."

BMGT 273

INTERNATIONAL CONSUMER BEHAVIOR

Course:	BMGT 273 International Consumer Behavior
Semester:	Spring of every year
Credits:	Credits: 3
Description:	Analysis and application of consumer behavior theory and models in international retailing. Behavioral and cross cultural research and theoretical issues in the global marketplace. Purchasing patterns, mall rat culture and five finger discounts are additionally explored, mocked and "discounted."
Dates:	SUMMER - Open

"A boy was walking down the street when all of a sudden he turned into a store." That little chestnut may just have been the first joke many of us learned. I know it was mine. Of course, I was seventeen and, due to an astounding amount of time spent increasing the GNP of Columbia; I didn't get it. But shopping jokes are a normal Rockwell-esque piece of Americana that should be passed down from generation to generation. Or your can tell the jokes below and end it now.

—*Steve*

A married couple was on holiday in Jamaica. They were touring around the marketplace looking at the goods and such when they passed this small sandal shop. From inside, they heard the shopkeeper with a Jamaican accent say, "You foreigners! Come in. Come into my humble shop!" So the married couple walked in.

The Jamaican said to them, "I have some special sandals I think you would be interested in. Dey make you wild at sex." The wife was really interested in buying the sandals after what the man claimed, but her husband felt he really didn't need them, being the sex god he was.

The husband asked the man, "How could sandals make you into a sex freak?"

The Jamaican replied, "Just try dem on, Mon." The husband, after some badgering from his wife, finally gave in, and tried them on. As soon as he slipped them his feet, he got this wild look in his eyes. . . something his wife hadn't seen in many years! In the blink of an eye, the husband grabbed the Jamaican, bent him violently over a table, yanked down his pants, ripped down his own pants, and grabbed a firm hold of the Jamaican's hips.

The Jamaican then began screaming, "YOU GOT DEM ON DE WRONG FEET! YOU GOT DEM ON DE WRONG FEET, MON!"

* * * *

A guy walks into a supermarket and buys the following items: one toothbrush, one tube of toothpaste, one roll of toilet paper, one frozen dinner, one can of pop, one box of cereal. The woman behind the counter says, "So you are single, huh?"

The man replies very sarcastically, "Why would you guess that, because I am buying one of everything?"

The woman replies, "No, because you're ugly."

* * * *

Bubba was fixing a door and he found that he needed a new hinge, so he sent Mary Louise to the hardware store. At the hardware store, Mary Louise saw a great toaster on a top shelf while she was waiting for Joe Bob to finish waiting on a customer. When Joe Bob was finished, Mary Louise asked, "How much for the toaster?"

Joe Bob replied "That's silver, and it costs $100!"

"My goodness, that sure is a lotta money!" Mary Louise exclaimed.

She then proceeded to describe the hinge that Bubba had sent her to buy, and Jo Bob went to the backroom to find a hinge.

From the backroom, Joe Bob yelled "Mary Louise, you wanna screw for that hinge?"

To which Mary Louise replied, "No, but I'll blow you for the toaster!"

A man who had a hairlip stopped to buy some peanuts from a peanut vendor. He asked, "How much are your cashews?"

The peanut vendor, who had a humpback, replied "Eight dollars a pound."

"Eight dollars?!?" cried the hairlip man. "That's too high. How much are your pistachios?"

The humpbacked vendor replied, "Ten dollars a pound."

"Ten dollars?!?" cried the hairlip man, "That's too high. How much are your Spanish peanuts?"

The humpback vendor said, "Two dollars a pound."

The hairlip man said he wanted a quarter pound of the Spanish peanuts. After paying for the peanuts, the hairlip man said, "I want to thank you for not making fun of my hairlip." The peanut vendor replied, "That's okay, I want to thank you for not making fun of my humpback."

The hairlip man said, "Humpback! I thought that was your ass, since your nuts were so high!"

* * * *

A man walks into a drug store with his 8-year-old son. They happen to walk by the condom display, and the boy asks, "What are these, Dad?"

To which the man matter-of-factly replies, "Those are called condoms, son. Men use them to have safe sex."

"Oh I see," replied the boy pensively. "Yes, I've heard of that in health class at school." He looks over the display and picks up a package of 3 and asks, "Why are there 3 in this package?"

The dad replies, "Those are for high school boys: ONE for Friday, ONE for Saturday, and ONE for Sunday."

"Cool," says the boy. He notices a 6-pack and asks, "Then who are these for?"

"Those are for college men, " the dad answers: TWO for Friday, TWO for Saturday, and TWO for Sunday."

"WOW!" exclaimed the boy. "Then who uses THESE?" he asks, picking up a 12-pack.

With a sigh and a tear in his eye, the dad replied, "Those are for the married men: ONE for January, ONE for February, ONE for March . . ."

* * * *

A store that sells new husbands has just opened in New York City, where a woman may go to choose a husband. Among the instructions at the entrance is a description of how the store operates. "You may visit the store ONLY ONCE! There are six floors and the attributes of the men increase as the shopper ascends the flights. There is, however, a catch: you may choose any man from a particular floor, or you may choose to go up a floor, but you cannot go back down except to exit the building.

So, a woman goes to the Husband Store to find a husband. On the first floor the sign on the door reads: Floor 1 - These men have jobs. "The second floor sign reads: Floor 2 - These men have jobs and love kids.

The third floor sign reads: Floor 3 - These men have jobs, love kids, and are extremely good looking.

"Wow," she thinks, but feels compelled to keep going. She goes to the fourth floor and sign reads: Floor 4 - These men have jobs, love kids, are drop-dead good looking and help with the housework.

"Oh, mercy me!" she exclaims, "I can hardly stand it."

Still, she goes to the fifth floor and sign reads: Floor 5 - These men have jobs, love kids, are drop-dead gorgeous, help with the housework, and have a strong romantic streak.

She is so tempted to stay, but she goes to the sixth floor and the sign reads: Floor 6 - You are visitor 31,456,012 to this floor. There are no men on this floor. This floor exists solely as proof that women are impossible to please. Thank you for shopping at the Husband Store. "

* * * *

A New Wives store opened across the street.

The first floor has wives that love sex. "The second floor has wives that love sex and have money. "The third through sixth floors have never been visited."

* * * *

A sixty-year-old man walks into a drug store and walks up to the girl at the checkout counter. He asks her, "Do you sell condoms here?"

"Sure. What size are you?"

"I don't know," he replies.

"Well, just let me check," the cashier says. She unzips his pants, takes a feel, and then says over the intercom, "Extra large condoms to the checkout counter please. Extra large condoms to the checkout counter."

A clerk returns with some condoms. The man pays for them and leaves the store.

Later, a thirty-year-old man walks into the store and up to the checkout counter. He asks the girl, "Do you sell condoms here?"

The cashier replies, "Sure. What size do you need?"

"Well, I don't know."

"Allow me to check for you," she says as she unzips his pants and takes a couple of tugs. She then says over the intercom, "Large condoms to the checkout counter please. Large condoms to the checkout counter." A clerk returns with some condoms. The man pays for them and leaves the store.

Some time later, a fifteen-year-old boy, hoping to get lucky, walks up to the girl at the checkout counter and asks sheepishly, "Um, ah, do you guys sell condoms here?"

"Yep," she says. "What size do you need?"

"I don't know," he says nervously.

"Allow me to check for you," she says. The cashier unzips his pants for a feel, pauses for a moment and then says over the intercom, "Clean up at the checkout counter please. Clean up at the checkout counter."

* * * *

A blonde sorority girl walks into a pharmacy and asks the assistant for some rectum deodorant. The pharmacist, a little bemused, explains to the girl they don't sell rectum deodorant and never have. Unfazed, she assures the pharmacist that she has been buying the stuff from this store on a regular basis and would like some more. "I'm sorry", says the pharmacist, "we don't have any."

"But I always buy it here," says the blonde.

"Do you have the container that it came in?" asks the pharmacist.

"Yes", said the blonde, "I'll go home and get it."

She returns with the container and hands it to the pharmacist who looks at it and says to her, "This is just a normal stick of underarm deodorant."

Annoyed, she snatches the container back and reads out loud from the container, "TO APPLY, PUSH UP BOTTOM."

* * * *

A woman goes into a sports store to buy a rod and reel for her grandson's birthday. She doesn't know which one to get, so she just grabs one and goes over to the salesman who is wearing sunglasses. She says, "Excuse me. Can you tell me anything about this rod and reel?"

He says, "Madam, I'm completely blind. But if you'll drop it on the counter, I can tell you everything you need to know about it from the sound it makes."

She doesn't believe him but drops it on the counter anyway. He says, "That's a six-foot Shakespeare graphite rod with a Zebco 404 reel and 10-lb. test line. It's on sale this week for $44."

She says, "It's amazing that you can tell all that just by the sound of it dropping on the counter. I'll take it!" As she opens her purse her credit card drops on the floor.

"Oh, that sounds like a Visa card," he says. As the lady bends down to pick up the card, she accidentally farts. At first she is really embarrassed but then realizes there is no way the blind salesman could tell it was she who had farted. The man rings up the sale and says, "That'll be $58.50 please."

The woman is totally confused by this and asks, "Didn't you tell me it was on sale for $44. How did you get to $58.50?"

"The duck caller is $11 and the fish bait is $3.50"

* * * *

A lady walked into a Lexus dealership just to browse. Suddenly, she spotted the most beautiful car that she had ever seen and walked over to inspect it. As she bent forward to feel the fine leather upholstery, an unexpected little fart escaped her. Embarrassed, she anxiously looked around to see if anyone had noticed and hoped a sales person didn't pop up right now.

But, as she turned back, there, standing next to her, is a salesman. With a pleasant smile he greeted her, "Good day, Madame. How may we help you today?"

Trying to maintain an air of sophistication and acting as though nothing had happened, she smiled back and asked, "Sir, what is the price of this lovely vehicle?"

Still smiling pleasantly, he replied, "Madame, I'm very sorry to say that if just touching it made you fart, you are going to shit when you hear the price."

* * * *

A young man walked into a jeweler's shop late one Friday with a stunning young lady at his side.

"I'm looking for a special ring for my girl friend," he said. The jeweler looked through his stock, and took out an outstanding ring priced at $5,000.

"I don't think you understand. I want something very unique," the young man said.

At that, the jeweler fetched his special stock from the safe. "Here's one stunning ring I had kept for the princess. Since you want something special for the stunning lady I will give it to you for $40,000."

The young lady's eyes lit up and started to sparkle. Seeing this, the young man said he would take it.

"How are you paying, sir?"

"I will pay by check. But, of course the bank would want to make sure that everything is in order, so, I will write the check now and you can phone the bank tomorrow. Then I will pick up the ring on Monday. Is that okay with you?" the young man asked. The jeweler agreed.

Monday morning, a very pissed off jeweler phoned the young man. "You fraud! You lied. There is no money in that account!"

"I know, but can you imagine what a fantastic weekend I had?"

* * * *

It had been many years since the embarrassing day when a young woman, baby in arm, entered the butcher shop and confronted the owner with the news that the baby was his, and what was he going to do about it?

The butcher offered to give her free meat until the boy was 16 and the woman agreed.

The butcher had been counting off the years on his calendar until one day, the teenager, who had been coming in to collect the meat each week, boasted to the butcher, "I'll be 16 tomorrow."

"I know," said the butcher with a smile.

"I've been waiting for this day for a long time. Tell your mother, when you take this parcel of meat home, that it is the last free meat she'll get. Watch the expression on her face."

The boy took the meat home and told his mother what the butcher had said.

Mother nodded and said, "Son, go back to the butcher and tell him I have also had free bread, free milk, and free groceries for the last 16 years. And watch the expression on HIS face!"

* * * *

The couple had been debating the purchase of a new auto for weeks. He wanted a new truck. She wanted a fast little sports car so she could zip through traffic around town. He would probably have settled on any beat up old truck, but everything she seemed to like was way out of their price range. "Look!" she said. "I want something that goes from 0 to 200 in 4 seconds or less. And my birthday is coming up. You could surprise me."

For her birthday, he bought her a brand new bathroom scale.

* * * *

This guy has always dreamed of owning a Harley Davidson. One day he has finally saved up enough money, so he goes down to the dealer. After he picks out the perfect bike, the dealer tells him about an old biker trick that will keep the chrome on his new bike free from rust. The dealer tells him that all he has to do is to keep a jar of Vaseline handy and put it on the chrome before it rains, and everything will be fine.

A few months later, the young man meets a woman and falls in love. She asks him to come home and meet her parents over dinner. He readily accepts, and the date is set. At the appointed time, he picks her up on his Harley and they ride to her parents' house.

Before they go in, she tells him that they have a family tradition that whoever speaks first after dinner does the dishes. After a delicious dinner, everyone sits in silence waiting for the first person to break the silence and get stuck doing the dishes. After a long fifteen minutes, the young man decides to speed things up, so he reaches over and kisses his woman in front of her family. No one says a word.

Emboldened, he slips his hand under her blouse and fondles her breasts. Still no one says a word. Finally, he throws her on the table and has sex with her in front of everyone. No one says a word. Now he is getting desperate, so he grabs her mother and throws HER on the table. They have even wilder sex. Still no one speaks.

By now he is thinking what to do next when he hears thunder in the distance. His first thought is to protect the chrome on his Harley, so he gets his jacket, reaches in his pocket and pulls out his jar of Vaseline.

The father says, "Okay dammit, I'll do the dishes!"

* * * *

A doctor goes out and buys the best car on the market, a brand new Ferrari GTO. It is also the most expensive car in the world, and it costs him $500,000. He takes it out for a spin and stops at a red light.

An old man on a moped, looking about 100 years old, pulls up next to him. The old man looks over at the sleek, shiny car and asks, "What kind of car ya got there, sonny?"

The doctor replies, "A Ferrari GTO. It cost half a million dollars!"

"That's a lot of money," says the old man. "Why does it cost so much?"

"Because this car can do up to 320 miles an hour!" states the doctor proudly.

The Moped driver asks, "Mind if I take a look inside?"

"No problem," replies the doctor.

So the old man pokes his head in the window and looks around.

Then, sitting back on his Moped, the old man says, "That's a pretty nice car, all right ... but I'll stick with my moped!"

Just then the light changes, so the doctor decides to show the old man just what his car can do. He floors it, and within 30 seconds, the speedometer reads 160 mph. Suddenly, he notices a dot in his rear view mirror. It seems to be getting closer. He slows down to see what it could be and suddenly WHOOSH! Something whips by him going much faster!

"What on earth could be going faster than my Ferrari?" the doctor asks himself. He floors the accelerator and takes the Ferrari up to 250 mph. Then, up ahead of him, he sees that it's the old man on the moped!

Amazed that the moped could pass his Ferrari, he gives it more gas and passes the moped at 275 mph.

He's feeling pretty good until he looks in his mirror and sees the old man gaining on him AGAIN! Astounded by the speed of this old guy, he floors the gas pedal and takes the Ferrari all the way up to 320 mph. Not ten seconds later, he sees the moped bearing down on him again!

The Ferrari is flat out, and there's nothing he can do! Suddenly, the moped plows into the back of his Ferrari, demolishing the rear end. The doctor stops and jumps out and unbelievably the old man is still alive.

He runs up to the mangled old man and says, "Oh My Gosh! Is there anything I can do for you?"

The old man whispers, "Unhook ... my suspenders ... from your ... side view ... mirror."

* * * *

A little old lady, well into her eighties, slowly enters the front door of a sex shop. Obviously very unstable on her feet, she wobbles the few feet across the store to the counter. Finally arriving at the counter and grabbing it for support, stuttering, she asks the sales clerk, "D-d-dooo y-y-youuuu h-h-have d-d-d-dildosss?"

The clerk, politely trying not to burst out laughing, replies, "Yes we do have dildos. Actually we carry many different models."

"The old woman then asks, "D-d-doooo y-y-youuu c-carrryy a-a-a p-p-pinkk onnne, t-t-tennn inchessss l-l-long a-a-andd a-abouttt t-twooo inchesss th-thiicklk . . . a-a-and r-runnsss b-by b-baatteries?"

The clerk responds, "Yes we do."

"D-d-d-dooo y-yoooouuuu kn-knoooww h-h-howww t-t-tooo t-t-turrrnnn i-i-itttt o-offfff?"

* * * *

A rich man and a poor man are sitting at a table together just after Christmas at some benefit. The poor man, trying to make conversation, asks the rich man what he gave his wife for Christmas.

"Well," the rich man replies, "I went to the most expensive jewelry store and bought her a diamond ring and then went to the classiest car dealership and got her a Mercedes Benz."

"Wow," the poor man says, "why did you get her both?"

"Well," says the rich man, "if she doesn't like the ring, she can always jump in her Benz and take it back."

The rich man asks the poor man what he gave his wife for Christmas.

The poor man says, "I gave her a pair of slippers and a dildo."

The rich man says, "That's an odd combination. Why both?"

"Well, "the poor man says, "if she doesn't like the slippers, she can go screw herself."

* * * *

A husband and wife were having difficulty surviving financially, so they decided that the wife should try prostitution as an extra source of income. The husband drove her out to a popular corner and informed her he would be at the side of the building if she had any questions or problems.

A gentleman pulled up shortly after and asked her how much to go all the way. She told him to wait a minute and ran around the corner to ask her husband. The husband told her to tell the client $100.

She went back and informed the client at which he cried, "That's too much!" He then asked, "How much for a handjob?"

She asked him to wait a minute and ran to ask her husband how much to charge. The husband said, "Ask for $40".

The woman ran back and informed the client. He felt that this was an agreeable price and began to remove his pants and underwear. Upon the removal of his clothing the woman noticed that the man was really well-hung. She asked him once more to wait a moment. She ran around the corner again at which her husband asked, "Now what?"

The wife replied, "Can I borrow $60?"

* * * *

Guy goes into a drug store and asks for some cough mixture. The assistant gave him a bottle of extra-strength laxative, much to his surprise. "This is no good," he said. "I want cough mixture."

To this the chemist replied, "Take my word for it sir, one dose of that and you won't dare cough."

* * * *

Finally, a definition of Marketing that makes sense...

You see a gorgeous girl at a party. You go up to her and say, "I'm fantastic in bed."

That's Direct Marketing.

You're at a party with a bunch of friends and see a gorgeous girl. One of your friends goes up to her and pointing at you says, "He's fantastic in bed."

That's Advertising.

You see a gorgeous girl at a party. You go up to her and get her telephone number. The next day you call and say, "Hi, I'm fantastic in bed."

That's Telemarketing.

You're at a party and see a gorgeous girl. You get up and straighten your tie, you walk up to her and pour her a drink. You open the door for her, pick up her bag after she drops it, offer her a ride, and then say, "By the way, I'm fantastic in bed."

That's Public Relations.

You're at a party and see a gorgeous girl. She walks up to you and says, "I hear you're fantastic in bed."

That's Brand Recognition.

* * * *

A young man hired by a supermarket reported for his first day of work. The manager greeted him with a warm handshake and a smile, gave him a broom, and said, "Your first job will be to sweep out the store."

"But I'm a college graduate," the young man replied indignantly."

"Oh, I'm sorry. I didn't realize that," said the manager. "Here, give me the broom — I'll show you how."

* * * *

Crazy Mike the Biker walks into a pharmacy and says to the pharmacist, "Listen, I have three girls coming over tonight. I've never had three girls at once, and I need something to keep me horny ... keep me potent."

The pharmacist reaches under the counter, unlocks the bottom drawer and takes out a small cardboard box marked with a label "Viagra Extra Strength" and says, "Here, if you eat this, you'll go NUTS for 12 hours!"

Then Crazy Mike says, "Gimme three boxes!" The next day, Crazy Mike walks into the same pharmacy, right up to the same pharmacist and pulls down his pants. The pharmacist looks in horror as he notices the man's penis is black and blue, and the skin is hanging off in some places.

Crazy Mike says, "Gimme a bottle of BenGay."

The pharmacist replies, "BenGay?!? You're not going to put BenGay on that are you?"

Crazy Mike says, "No, it's for my arms, the girls didn't show up."

* * * *

A traveling salesman knocks on the door of a house and after a few seconds the door is opened by a ten-year-old boy wearing a pink tutu and holding a martini in one hand and a cigar in the other.

Naturally the salesman is taken aback by this sight, and when he composes himself, asks, "Excuse me young man but are your parents home?"

The boy takes a puff on his cigar, looks up at the salesman and says, "What do you fuckin' think?"

* * * *

A shy guy goes into a bar and sees a beautiful woman sitting at the bar. After an hour of gathering up his courage he finally goes over to her and asks, tentatively, "Um, would you mind if I chatted with you for a while?"

She responds by yelling, at the top of her lungs, "No, I won't sleep with you tonight!" Everyone in the bar is now staring at them. Naturally, the guy is hopelessly and completely embarrassed and he slinks back to his table.

After a few minutes, the woman walks over to him and apologizes. She smiles at him and says, "I'm sorry if I embarrassed you. You see, I'm a graduate student in psychology and I'm studying how people respond to embarrassing situations." To which he responds, at the top of his lungs, "What do you mean $200?"

JOKE ANALYSIS
BY DR. BROWN

Though Madonna is wrong in virtually every category, including style, taste, tone, pitch, and scent (one assumes), she was correct in her assertion that "we are living in a material world." Though a certain American predisposition can be identified with regards to ephemera most consumed, the influence of native cultures can also be found in the items people choose to covet.

The following was repeated with great amusement by Tony, a greasy middle-aged pizza spinner who pines insanely for the old country, which for him would be Sheepshead Bay, Brooklyn, from which he has never ventured.

"Giorgio is in this country for about six months. He walks to work every day and passes a shoe store. Each day he stops and looks in the window and admires a certain pair of Bocceli leather shoes.

After about two months he saves the $300 the shoes cost and purchases them.

Each Friday night the Italian community gets together at a dance at the church basement, so Giorgio seizes the opportunity to wear his new Bocceli leather shoes to the dance. He asks Sophia to dance and as they dance he asks her, "Sophia, do you wear red panties tonight?" Sophia, startled, says, "Yes, Giorgio, I do wear red panties tonight, but how do you know?" Giorgio replies, "I see-a the reflection in-a my new $300 Bocceli leather shoes. How do you like them?"

Next he asks Rosa to dance, after a few minutes he says to her, "Rosa, do you wear white panties tonight?" Rosa answers, "Yes, Giorgio, I do, but how do you know that?" He answers, "I see-a the reflection in-a my new $300 Bocceli leather shoes. How do you like them?"

Now the evening is almost over and the last song is being played, so Giorgio asks Carmella to dance. Midway through the dance his face turns red. He says, "Carmella, stilla my heart. Please, please tell me you wear no panties tonight. Please, please, tella me this true."

Carmella answers, "Yes Giorgio, I wear no panties tonight."

Giorgio gasps and says, "Thank-a God . . . I thought I had a crack in-a my $300 Bocelli leather shoes."

Tony makes a glaring error that reveals a profound lack of knowledge about our friends from the boot of Europe. For, while it is perfectly plausible that Carmella would have eschewed undergarments, it is unthinkable that Giorgio could have mistaken this for a crack in his shoes.

Italian women, born as they are with mustaches that would do a Mexican Bandit proud, need never worry about unintentional vaginal exposure. By the time they reach sexual maturity, at the age of 9, their genitalia are completely covered by a lush layer of fur reminiscent of 1970's-era vintage pornography. And by the time they are attending church socials, even a seasoned jungle explorer might be daunted at the prospect of approaching a Bella Donna's holiest of holies without a machete to hack through the dense foliage.

Thus, a more accurate punchline might read:

"Thank-a God, I thought-a Marv Albert's Toupee had escaped and attacked my-a $300 Bocelli Shoes"

Yet even that modification cannot save the joke, for it doesn't address the inconsistency of Giorgio's behavior.

As an Italian-American man, one can be sure that Giorgio would not have paid $300 for his beloved shoes. Rather, they would have conveniently "fallen out of a truck" in just the right size. As such "accidents" can happen at any time, it is unlikely that Giorgio would have felt such an attachment towards his footwear. Indeed, recent studies have suggested that Italian men are genetically incapable of feeling affection towards anything other than their mother.

Finally, I would like to take this opportunity to inform National Lampoon readers that even a non-Paisano can pick up a nice pair of Bostonian Bocelli shoes for a mere $100 at www.shoesonlinestore.com. Remember, with their soft, supple leather uppers and unique stitched construction combining durability and flexibility, a Bocelli loafer is a perfect contemporary design for a variety of occasions.

ATHL 456
ETHICAL ISSUES
IN ATHLETICS

Course:	ATHL 456 Ethical Issues in Athletics
Semester:	Summer of every year
Credits:	2
Restrictions:	Not open to freshmen or sophomores.
Description:	Ethics of sports at the institutional level in contemporary society. Political, social, and commercial pressures. Matters of urine substitution, cheerleader buggery. Peripheral competitions such as locker room towel snapping.
Dates:	SPRING - Open

Let's get one thing straight; being athletic is easy, sounding athletic is an art. That is why I, and many like me, train rigorously for the time honored tradition of sports joking. A laugh in the locker room will always trump a mediocre performance on the field. In fact, I no longer play — I just hang around in the locker room telling jokes. I can tell the other guys are intimidated by my cleverness; they all act real edgy and weird around me before I've even said anything.

—*Steve*

A woman is picked up by Dennis Rodman in a bar. They like each other and she goes back with him to his hotel room. He removes his shirt revealing all his tattoos and she sees that on his arm is one which reads, "Reebok." She thinks that is a bit odd and asks him about it.

Dennis says, "When I play basketball, the cameras pick up the tattoo and Reebok pays me for advertisement." A bit later, his pants are off and she sees "Puma" tattooed on his leg. He gives the same explanation for the unusual tattoo. Finally, the underwear comes off and she sees the word "AIDS" tattooed on his penis. She jumps back with shock.

"I'm not going to do it with a guy who has AIDS!"

He says, "Relax baby. In a minute it's going to say 'ADIDAS'."

* * * *

A bunch of guys are in the locker room at their golf club. A cell phone on a bench rings, and one of the guys engages the hands-free speaker function and begins to talk. Everyone else in the room stops to listen. You would too, right?

MAN: Hello.

WOMAN: Honey, its me. Are you at the club?

MAN: Yes.

WOMAN: I am at the mall now and found this beautiful leather coat. Its only $1,000. Is it okay if I buy it?

MAN: Sure, go ahead if you like it that much.

WOMAN: I also stopped by the Mercedes dealership and saw the new models. I saw one I really liked.

MAN: How much?

WOMAN: $90,000.

MAN: Okay, but for that price I want it with all the options.

WOMAN: Great! Oh, and one more thing . . . the house I wanted last year is back on the market. They're asking $950,000.

MAN: Well, then go ahead and give them an offer of $900,000. They will probably take it. If not, we can go the extra $50,000. It's a pretty good price.

WOMAN: Okay. I'll see you later! I love you so much!!

MAN: Bye! I love you, too.

He hangs up. The other men in the locker room are staring at him in astonishment, mouths agape.

The guy smiles and asks, "Anyone know whose phone this is?"

* * * *

A couple of women were playing golf one sunny Saturday morning. The first of the twosome teed off and watched in horror as her ball headed directly toward a foursome of men playing the next hole. She yelled "fore," but it was too late.

The ball hit one of the men and he immediately clasped his hands together at his crotch, fell to the ground and proceeded to roll around in obvious agony. The woman rushed over to the man and immediately began to apologize. "Please allow me to help. I'm a physical therapist and I know I could relieve your pain if you'd allow me, " she told him earnestly.

"Ummph, oooh, noooo... I'll be fine in a few minutes," he replied breathlessly as he remained in the fetal position still clasping his hands together at his crotch.

But she persisted, and he finally allowed her to help him. She gently took his hands away and laid them to the side. She loosened his pants, and put her hands inside. She began to massage his privates. She then asked him, "How does that feel?"

He replied still in agony, "Great, but you hit my thumb!"

* * * *

Two cowboys are out on the range talking about their favorite sex positions: One says, "I think I enjoy the rodeo position the best."

"I don't think I have ever heard of that one," says the other cowboy, "what is it?"

"Well, it's where you get your girlfriend down on all fours, and you mount her from behind, and you reach around and cup each one of her breasts in your hands, and then you whisper in her ear, 'Boy, these feel just like your sister's' and then you try to hold on for 8 seconds."

* * * *

John was a wrestler who had worked his way to the finals. This is for the championship of the world. His coach tells him that the Russian champ has a special hold. He goes on to say the Russian Cork Screw is his best hold. The coach tells John that no one has ever gotten out of this hold. So he told John, "Whatever you do, keep away from that hold!" The match starts and John is holding his own and has the edge. All of a sudden, the Russian gets John in the Russian Cork Screw.

The coach cannot stand to watch and walks to the dressing room area. Moments later he hears a load cheer of "USA! USA!" He runs back to see them holding John's hand in victory. After they are back in the dressing room, the coach asked, "How did you get out of his hold?"

John replied, "Well, I was all twisted up and I saw two testicles hanging over my mouth."

"So I asked myself, 'What do I have to lose?' So I bit down hard on the testicles," John said, "and you will never know how strong you are until, you bite your own nuts!"

* * * *

A couple loved to golf together, but neither of them is playing like they want to, so they decide to take private lessons. The guy has his lesson first. After the pro sees his swing, he says, "No, no, no, you're gripping the club way too hard!"

"Well, what should I do?" asks the guy.

"Hold the club gently," the pro replied, "just like you'd hold your girlfriend's breast." The man takes the advice, takes a swing, and WOW! He hits the ball 250 yards, straight up the fairway. He goes back to his girlfriend with the good news, and she can't wait for her lesson.

The next day the girl goes for her lesson. The pro watches her swing and says, "No, no, no, you're gripping the club way too hard."

"What can I do?" she asks.

"Hold the club gently, just like you'd hold your boyfriend's penis." The girl listens carefully to the pro's advice, takes a swing, and THUMP. The ball goes straight down the fairway . . . about 15 feet.

"That was great," the pro says. "Now, take the club out of your mouth and swing the club like you're supposed to!"

* * * *

A married professor was having an affair with his pretty young student. One day they went to her place and made love all afternoon. Exhausted, they fell asleep and woke up at 8 PM. The professor hurriedly dressed and told the student to take his shoes outside and rub them in the grass and dirt. He put on his shoes and drove home.

"Where have you been?" his wife demanded.

"I can't lie to you." he replied, "I'm having an affair with one of my students. We had sex all afternoon."

She looked down at his shoes and said: "You lying bastard! You've been playing golf!"

* * * *

A blonde wanted to go ice fishing. She'd seen many books on the subject, and finally getting all the necessary tools together, she made for the ice. After positioning her comfy footstool, she started to make a circular cut in the ice. Suddenly, from the sky, a voice boomed, "THERE ARE NO FISH UNDER THE ICE." Startled, the blonde moved further down the ice, poured a thermos of cappuccino, and began to cut yet another hole. Again from the heavens the voice bellowed, "THERE ARE NO FISH UNDER THE ICE." The blonde, now worried, moved away, clear down to the opposite end of the ice. She set up her stool once more and tried again to cut her hole. The voice came once more, "THERE ARE NO FISH UNDER THE ICE."

She stopped, looked skyward, and said, "Is that you, Lord?"

The voice replied, "NO, THIS IS THE MANAGER OF THE HOCKEY RINK."

* * * *

A boss says to an underling: "I'm off to Sault Ste. Marie for the weekend."

"Sault Ste. Marie?" asks the employee, incredulous. "But, boss, there's nothing but whores and hockey players in Sault Ste. Marie."

"My wife is from Sault Ste. Marie."

"Oh. What position does she play?"

* * * *

Two sportsmen are hiking in the forest when they suddenly come across a big grizzly bear! The one guy takes off his hiking boots and puts on some running shoes! His friend says to him "You're crazy! There's no use. Do you know how fast grizzlies are, you'll never be able to outrun it!"

And the guy says, "I only have to outrun you!"

* * * *

Two old friends were just about to tee off at the first hole of their local golf course when a guy carrying golf bag called out to them, "Do you mind if I join you? My partner didn't turn up."

"Sure," they said, "You're welcome."

So they started playing and enjoyed the game and the company of the newcomer. Part way around the course, one of the friends asked the newcomer, "What do you do for a living?"

"I'm a hit man," was the reply.

"You're joking!" was the response.

"No, I'm not," he said, reaching into his golf bag and pulling out a beautiful Martini sniper's rifle with a large telescopic sight. "Here are my tools."

"That's a beautiful telescopic sight," said the other friend, "Can I take a look? I think I might be able to see my house from here."

So he picked up the rifle and looked through the sight in the direction of his house. "Yeah, I can see my house all right. This sight is fantastic. I can see right in the window. Wow, I can see my wife in the bedroom. Ha Ha, I can see she's naked!! Wait a minute, that's my neighbor in there with her...... He's naked, too!!! The bitch!"

He turned to the hit man, "How much do you charge for a hit?"

"I'll do a flat rate, for you, one thousand dollars every time I pull the trigger."

"Can you do two for me now?"

"Sure, what do you want?"

"First, shoot my wife. She's always been mouthy, so shoot her in the mouth."

"Then the neighbor, he's a friend of mine, so just shoot his dick off to teach him a lesson."

The hit man took the rifle and took aim, standing perfectly still for a few minutes.

"Are you going to do it or not?" said the friend impatiently.

"Just be patient, "said the hit man calmly, "I think I can save you a thousand dollars."

* * * *

A guy named Bob receives a free ticket to the Superbowl from his company. Unfortunately, when Bob arrives at the stadium, he realizes the seat is in the last row in the corner of the stadium. He is closer to the Goodyear Blimp than the field. About halfway through the first quarter, Bob notices an empty seat 10 rows off the field, right on the 50-yard line.

He decides to take a chance and makes his way through the stadium and around the security guards to the empty seat. As he sits down, he asks the gentleman sitting next to him, "Excuse me, is anyone sitting here?" The man says no.

Now, very excited to be in such a great seat for the game, Bob again inquires of the man next to him, "This is incredible! Who in their right mind would have a seat like this at the Superbowl and not use it?"

The man replies, "Well, actually, the seat belongs to me. I was supposed to come with my wife, but she passed away. This is the first Superbowl we haven't been to together since we got married in 1967."

"Well, that's really sad," says Bob, "but still, couldn't you find someone to take the seat? A relative or a close friend?"

"No, "the man replies, "they're all at the funeral."

* * * *

One fine sunny day, Jesus, Moses, and an old man are getting ready to tee off on the first hole.

Jesus is the first to tee off, and after a couple of quick practice swings, he smacks the ball into the air. As it flies from the tee, the ball heads straight towards the water trap. The ball plummets downwards, landing right in the middle of the water.

Rather than sinking to the bottom, however, the ball bounces off the surface of the water, then bounces again and again, almost walking on the surface of the water, until it rolls back onto land and right up to the edge of the green. Moses walks up, pats him on the back, and says "Nice shot, Jesus."

Now it's Moses' turn, and after a couple of quick practice swings, he lets it rip.

His ball also heads right towards the water trap, but hits ground a few feet before the water and starts rolling towards it. Just before the ball enters the water, the water parts right down the middle, leaving a clear path for the ball to roll along the bottom of the trap unobstructed. The ball rolls out the other side, the waters flow back together and the ball lands on the green, just a few feet from the pin. Jesus walks up, pats him on the back, and says "Nice shot, Moses!"

Finally, the old man steps up to the tee. Without so much as a warm-up swing, he hits the ball high into the air. Again, the ball heads right for the trap, and begins to drop towards the center of the water. Just before the ball splashes into the water, though, a turtle rises to the surface, and the ball bounces off the turtle shell, back into the air. The ball flies high back up into the air, and just as it reaches its peak and starts to drop back towards the water, a goose flies underneath and the ball lands on the back of the goose's neck. The goose flies away with the ball still on the back of his neck. Just as the goose flies over the green, a bolt of lightning strikes out of the clear blue sky, and the goose falls dead to the ground. The ball, now dislodged from the back of the goose, rolls gently across the green and into the hole.

Jesus says, "Hey Dad, you want fuck around or you want to play golf?"

＊ ＊ ＊ ＊

Don was so excited to be going bear hunting. He spotted a small brown bear in the woods and shot it. Then there was a tap on his shoulder. He turned around to see a big black bear. The black bear said, "Don, you've got two choices, either I maul you to death or we have rough sex." Don decided to bend over.

Even though he felt sore for two weeks, Don soon recovered and vowed revenge. He headed out on another trip where he found the black bear and shot it. There was another tap on his shoulder. This time a huge grizzly bear was standing right next to him. The grizzly said, "That was a huge mistake, Don. You've got two choices. Either I maul you to death, or we have rough sex." Again, Don thought it was better to comply.

Although he survived, it took several months before Don finally recovered. Outraged, he headed back to the woods, managed to track down the grizzly and shot it. He felt the sweet taste of revenge. But then there was a tap on his shoulder. Don turned round to find a giant polar bear standing there.

The polar bear said, "Admit it, you're not here for the hunting."

* * * *

A guy walked into a bar with his pet dog. The bartender said, "Sorry. No pets allowed."

The man replied, "This is a special dog. Turn on the Jets game and you'll see." The bartender, anxious to see what will happen, turned on the game.

The guy said, "Watch. Whenever the Jets score, my dog does flips." The Jets kept scoring field goals and the dog kept flipping and jumping.

"Wow! That's one hell of a dog you got there. What happens when the Jets score a touchdown?"

The man replied, "I don't know. I've only had him for seven years!"

* * * *

A man goes golfing with his friend, John. He arrives home several hours late. His wife asks," What took you so long?"

He replies, "Oh, honey, it was a horrible afternoon! On the third hole, John had a heart attack and died on the spot!"

She says, "Oh, darling! It must have been awful for you!"

The husband replies, "It was hell! Fifteen holes of hit the ball, drag John, hit the ball, drag John..."

* * * *

A man stumbles, dazed, into an emergency room with severe concussion, and a golf club wrapped round his neck several times.

The shocked doctor asks what happened.

The man, still very confused, describes a pleasant game of golf with his wife. "She swung, and hit the golf ball out of bounds and into a nearby field full of cattle" said the man. "Of course, we both went to find her ball. While looking around I noticed a cow with something white on its rear end. I lifted the tail, and recognized the ball as my wife's."

"What did you do next then?" asks the doctor?

"Well, feeling good about myself," the man replies, "I called to my wife: 'Hey this one looks like yours!' Then I woke up like this."

* * * *

A fellow walks into a bar, orders a drink, and asks the bartender if he'd like to hear a good Notre Dame joke.

"Listen buddy," he growled. "See those two big guys on your left? They were both linemen on the Notre Dame football team. And that huge fellow on your right was a world-class wrestler at Notre Dame. That guy in the corner was Notre Dame's all-time champion weight lifter. And I lettered in three sports at Notre Dame. Now, are you absolutely positive you want to go ahead and tell your joke here?"

"Nah, guess not," the man replied. "I wouldn't want to have to explain it 5 times."

* * * *

The huge college freshman figured he'd try out for the football team. "Can you tackle?" asked the coach.

"Watch this," said the freshman, who proceeded to run smack into a telephone pole, shattering it to splinters.

"Wow," said the coach. "I'm impressed. Can you run?"

"Of course I can run," said the freshman. He was off like a shot, and in just over nine seconds, he had run a hundred yard dash.

"Great!" enthused the coach. "But can you pass a football?"

The freshman rolled his eyes, hesitated for a few seconds. "Well, sir," he said, "if I can swallow it, I can probably pass it."

* * * *

As the woman passed her daughter's closed bedroom door, she heard a strange buzzing noise coming from within. Opening the door, she observed her daughter giving herself a real workout with a vibrator! Shocked, she asked, "What are you doing?"

The daughter replied, "Mom, I'm thirty-five years old, unmarried, and this thing is about as close as I'll ever get to a husband. Please go away and leave me alone."

The next day, the girl's father heard the same buzz coming from the other side of the closed bedroom door. Upon entering the room, he observed his daughter making passionate love to her vibrator.

To his query as to what she was doing, the daughter said, "Dad, I'm thirty-five years old, unmarried, and this thing is about as close as I'll ever get to a husband. Please go away and leave me alone."

A couple days later, the wife came home from a shopping trip, placed the groceries on the kitchen counter, and heard that buzzing noise coming from, of all places, the family room. She entered that area and observed her husband sitting on the couch, staring at the TV. The vibrator was next to him on the couch, buzzing away. The wife asked, "What the hell are you doing?

The husband replied, "Watching the ballgame with my son-in-law."

* * * *

A man was walking in the city, when he was accosted by a particularly dirty and shabby-looking bum who asked him for a couple of dollars for dinner. The man took out his wallet, extracted two dollars and asked, "If I gave you this money, will you take it and buy whiskey?"

"No, I stopped drinking years ago," the bum said.

"Will you use it to gamble?"

"I don't gamble. I need everything I can get just to stay alive."

"Will you spend the money on greens fees at a golf course?"

"Are you MAD? I haven't played golf in 20 years!"

The man said, "Well, I'm not going to give you two dollars. Instead, I'm going to take you to my home for a terrific dinner cooked by my wife."

The bum was astounded. "Won't your wife be furious with you for doing that? I know I'm dirty, and I probably smell pretty bad."

The man replied, "Hey, man, that's okay! I just want her to see what happens to a man who gives up drinking, gambling, and golf!"

* * * *

Three girls were sitting around talking about their sex lives.

The first said, "I think my boyfriend's like a championship golfer. He's spent the last ten years perfecting his stroke."

The second woman said, "My boyfriend's like the winner of the Indy 500. Every time we get into bed he gives me several hundred exciting laps."

The third woman was silent until she was asked, "Tell us about your boyfriend."

She thought for a moment and said, "My boyfriend's like an Olympic gold-medal-winning quarter-miler."

"How so?"

"He's got his time down to under 40 seconds."

* * * *

"Dear," said the wife. "What would you do if I died?"

"Why, dear, I would be extremely upset," said the husband. "Why do you ask such a question?"

"Would you remarry?" asked the wife.

"No, of course not, dear," said the husband.

"Don't you like being married?" said the wife.

"Of course I do, dear," he said.

"Then why wouldn't you remarry?" she asked.

"All right," said the husband, "I'd remarry."

"You would?" said the wife, looking vaguely hurt.

"Yes," said the husband.

"Would you sleep with her in our bed?" said the wife after a long pause.

"Well yes, I suppose I would." replied the husband.

"I see," said the wife indignantly. "And would you let her wear my old clothes?"

"I suppose, if she wanted to," said the husband.

"Really," said the wife icily.

"And would you take down the pictures of me and replace them with pictures of her?"

"Yes. I think that would be the correct thing to do."

"Is that so?" said the wife, leaping to her feet. "And I suppose you'd let her play with my golf clubs, too."

"Of course not, dear," said the husband. "She's left-handed!"

＊ ＊ ＊ ＊

A little bear is at his custody hearing. The judge asks the little bear whom he wants to live with.

"Well, I don't want to live with Mamma bear, she beats me. And I do not want to live with Papa Bear, he beats me too."

The judge asks little bear if he has any relatives whom he likes.

Little Bear says, "No. . . I want to live with the Chicago Bears, the don't beat anybody."

JOKE ANALYSIS
BY DR. BROWN

While the study of jokes is understood to be a higher calling offering no bias with regard to country of origin, there does appear to be an interesting phenomenon. In spite of a potato-bland lifestyle that provides extremely limited fodder for humor, the Irish seem to receive a disproportionate number of targeted jokes. This might be caused by their few activities (read; vices) being highly accessible to joke formulas, or because it is the only way to communicate a criticism without having to block a flurry of poorly aimed slaps and punches.

The reason the Irish are so defensive when criticized is largely unknown, but their ability to turn a personal jab into an issue of religious or national pride is legend. Virility is also a great cause celebre for the Irish as we see in this tall tale:

An Irishman moved to the USA and finally attended his first baseball game.

The first batter approached the batters' box, took a few swings and then hit a double.

Everyone was on their feet screaming "RUN! RUN!"

The next batter hit a single and the Irishman listened as the crowd again cheered, "RUN! RUN!"

The Irishman was enjoying the game (and a few beers of course) and began screaming with the fans.

The third batter came up and four balls went by. The umpire signaled a walk and the batter started his slow trot to first base.

Very much into the excitement of the game, the Irishman stood up and screamed, "R-R-Run ye s.o.b., run!"

The people around him began laughing. Embarrassed, the Irishman sat back down.

A friendly fan noted the man's embarrassment, leaned over and explained, "He can't run - he's got four balls."

The Irishman stood up and screamed, "Walk with pride, lad!"

Some may rightfully argue that to think an Irishman could enjoy a baseball game's-worth of beer without engaging in fisticuffs is as naive as believing that a Chicago White Sox fan could go nine innings without charging an umpire.

But to be fair, the Irishman in question is encouraging the third batter — which is early enough on in the proceedings that he might still be in his "happy" state. Indeed, soon our Irish friend may even propose a toast to the health of the whole stadium after sweet-talking his way into the jumbotron control room.

But make no doubt about it; by the 7th-inning stretch, he'll be reaching for his shillelagh. Traffic police in orange vests would be well-advised to watch their kneecaps.

DORM
LIFE

For most students, living in a dorm is their first experience living away from home. Life on the "quad" (or whatever you call your ghetto of higher education) is nothing like life at home. That is, unless your family likes to leave their shit everywhere, move your shit around, borrow your shit and not tell you about it, or sit on your head while you're sleeping and fart.

—*Steve*

Matt invited his mother over for dinner. During the meal, his mother eyed his beautiful roommate, suspicious that there was more than just a "roommate" situation going on. Matt saw her staring at Michelle. "I know what you're thinking, Mom, but Michelle and I are just friends." A week later, Michelle said, "Matt, ever since your mother came to dinner, I can't find the silver soup ladle. Surely she wouldn't have taken it, would she?"

"I really don't think so," Matt replied. "I'll write her a letter to ask, though." He got a sheet of paper, sat down, and wrote,

> "Dear Mom,
>
> I'm not saying you took our silver soup ladle, and I'm not saying you didn't take it.
>
> But our soup ladle has been missing ever since you came to dinner."

A few days later, he received a reply from his mother.

> "Dear son,
>
> I'm not saying that you are sleeping with Michelle, and I'm not saying that you are *not* sleeping with Michelle.
>
> But if she were sleeping in her own bed, she would have found the soup ladle by now.
>
> Love, Mom."

* * * *

A girl is in bed in her dorm room with her fuck buddy who also happens to be her boyfriend Bob's roommate. They make love for hours, and afterwards, while they're just laying there, the phone rings. Since it is the girl's room, she picks up the receiver. Her FB looks over at her and listens, only hearing her side of the conversation.

Speaking in a cheery voice, the girl says, "Hello? Oh, hi. I'm so glad that you called. Really? That's wonderful. I am so happy for you. That sounds terrific. Great! Thanks. Okay. Bye bye."

She hangs up the telephone and her FB asks, "Who was that?"

"Oh," she replies, "that was Bob telling me all about the wonderful time he's having on his fishing trip with you."

* * * *

A guy is having problems with premature ejaculation, so he goes to see his doctor. Doc says, "When you feel the urge to ejaculate, do something to startle yourself. That will distract you enough that the urge will pass."

So, the guy buys a starter's pistol and some blanks, then heads for his dorm room. By chance he finds his girlfriend nude, in bed waiting for him. They get down to business and are in the "69" position when he suddenly gets the urge. He picks up the pistol and fires a shot.

The next day he goes back to see the doctor, who asks, "How did it go?"

The guy says, "Not very well. When I fired the pistol, my girlfriend peed in my face, bit three inches off my penis and my roommate came out of the closet with his hands raised."

* * * *

My girlfriend and I were sitting in the living room and I said to her, "Just so you know, I never want to live in a vegetative state, dependent on some machine and fluids from a bottle. If that ever happens, just pull the plug."

She got up, unplugged the TV and threw out all of my beer!

* * * *

John receives a phone call. "Hello," he answers.

The voice on the other end says, "This is Susan. We met at a party in your dorm room about three months ago."

"Hmm . . . Susan? About 3 months ago?"

"Yes, it was at Bill's house. After the party you took me home. On the way we parked and got into the back seat. You told me I was a good sport."

"Oh, yeah! Susan! How are you?"

"I'm pregnant and I'm going to kill myself."

"Say, you ARE a good sport."

* * * *

A guy is nearing the end of his senior year in college. Unfortunately, he still has to share a room with his naive, virginal freshman roommate.

One night, he decides to bring his girlfriend home for a little fun. They have bunk beds and the guy notices that his roommate is already asleep on the lower bunk, so he and his girlfriend climb up to the top bunk. As you might expect, things start to heat up.

The guy remembers that his roommate is sleeping below so he tells his girlfriend to whisper "lettuce" if she wants it harder and "tomato" if she wants a new position.

"Lettuce!!! Tomato!!! Lettuce!!! Tomato!!! Lettuce!!! Tomato!!!" she screams.

"Lettuce!!! Tomato!!! Whoa!!! PULL IT OUT!!! PULL IT OUT NOW!!!"

Seconds later, the roommate shouts up, "Hey, would you guys stop making sandwiches up there? You're getting mayonnaise all over my face!"

* * * *

Two roommates were taking chemistry at the University of Alabama. They were so confident going into the final that two days before, they decided to go up to the University of Tennessee and party with some friends.

They had a great time. However, with hangovers and everything, they overslept and didn't make it back to Alabama until the morning of the exam. Rather than take the final, they found their professor afterward to explain why they missed the final.

They told him that they went up to the University of Tennessee for the weekend, and had planned to come back in time to study, but that they had a flat tire on the way back, and didn't have a spare, and couldn't get help for a long time, so they were late in getting back to campus.

The professor thought this over and told them they could make up the final on the following day. The two guys were elated and relieved. They studied that night and went in the next day for the final.

The professor placed them in separate rooms, and handed each of them a test booklet and told them to begin.

They looked at the first problem, which was worth five points. It was something simple. "Cool," they thought. "This is going to be easy." They did the first problem and then turned the page.

They were not prepared, however, for what they saw on this page.

"Which tire?? - 95 Points"

* * * *

A language instructor was explaining to her class that French nouns, unlike their English counterparts, are grammatically designated as masculine or feminine. Things like 'chalk' or 'pencil,' she described, would have a gender association although in English these words were neutral. Puzzled, one student raised his hand and asked, "What gender is a computer?"

The teacher wasn't certain which it was, and so divided the class into two groups and asked them to decide if a computer should be masculine or feminine. One group was composed of the women in the class, and the other, of men. Both groups were asked to give four reasons for their recommendation.

The group of women concluded that computers should be referred to in the masculine gender because:

1. In order to get their attention, you have to turn them on.

2. They have a lot of data but are still clueless.

3. They are supposed to help you solve your problems, but half the time they ARE the problem.

4. As soon as you commit to one, you realize that, if you had waited a little longer, you might have had a better model.

The men, on the other hand, decided that computers should definitely be referred to in the feminine gender because:

1. No one but their creator understands their internal logic.

2. The native language they use to communicate with other computers is incomprehensible to everyone else.

3. Even your smallest mistakes are stored in long-term memory for later retrieval.

4. As soon as you make a commitment to one, you find yourself spending half your paycheck on accessories for it.

* * * *

After thirty five years of carrying the mail through all kinds of weather to the same neighborhood, the mailman was going to retire. When he arrived at the first house on his route, he was greeted by the whole family who roundly and soundly congratulated him and sent him on his way with a tidy gift envelope.

At the second house, they presented him with a box of fine cigars.

The folks at the third house handed him a selection of terrific fishing lures.

At the fourth house he was met at the door by a strikingly beautiful woman in a revealing negligee. She took him by the hand, gently led him through the door and up the stairs to the bedroom where she blew his mind with the most passionate love he had ever experienced!

When he had enough, they went downstairs where she fixed him a giant breakfast; eggs, potatoes, ham, sausage, blueberry waffles, and fresh-squeezed orange juice.

When he was truly satisfied she poured him a cup of steaming coffee. As she was pouring, he noticed a dollar bill sticking out from under the cup's bottom edge.

"All of this was just too wonderful for words," he said. "But what's the dollar for?"

"Well," she said, "last night, I told my husband that today would be your last day, and that we should do something special for you. I asked him what to give you, and he said, 'Fuck him. Give him a dollar.' The breakfast was my idea!"

* * * *

A girl comes home to her dorm unexpectedly one day and finds her boyfriend in bed with a midget. Upset and furious over his actions, the woman screams, "You promised me two weeks ago that you would never cheat on me again!"

Trying his best to calm her down, the boyfriend turns to his wife and says, "Take it easy! Can't you see I'm trying to cut down?"

* * * *

The bank robbers arrived just before closing and promptly ordered the few remaining depositors, the tellers, clerks, and guards to disrobe and lie face down on the floor, behind the counter. One nervous blonde pulled off all her clothes and lay down on the floor facing upwards.

"Turn over, Cindy," whispered the girl lying beside her.

"This is a stick-up . . . not an frat party!"

JOKE ANALYSIS
BY DR. BROWN

There are several ways in which the term "Greek" can be applied. The nationality, the language, the culture of college fraternities and sororities, the list goes on and one. But, ultimately, all roads lead to ass fucking.

While refilling my pipe at a Chi Omega mixer in Utah where I was invited to speak on the subject of abstinence (an area of expertise foisted upon me by a steadfastly resistant universe), a Rubenesque young "virgin" surprised me with this blush-inducing joke.

Three members of the Delta Lambda Phi fraternity, a Jew, a Greek, and an Italian are walking down the street one fine day when sadly, their lives are interrupted by an out-of-control truck. Slamming into their bodies, the truck serves as their one-way trip to the Pearly Gates.

"Hmmm," says St. Peter, looking loftily over his books. "It looks as if this was a mistake; your time hasn't quite come yet. I'm gonna send you back. But I can't just do it and be done with it; I have to give you a stipulation: You have to refrain from doing your most favorite thing in the world."

The trio think it over, nod sagely and decide that this is acceptable for another chance at life. With a cloud of smoke, they are returned back to the street they disappeared from. Thanking their luck, they continue down the street.

Passing by a pizza parlor, the thick acrid smell of doughy tomatoes assaults all three's nostrils. The Italian, breaking out into a cold sweat, bolts for the doors, orders a slice, bites into it . . . and disappears in a puff of smoke.

The Jew and Greek, both observing this, exchange looks and continue on their way. The Jew spies a nickel on the sidewalk. He freezes, looks around, starts to sweat, starts to pick it up, stops, tries again, and finally when he can stand it no longer, he bends over to pick it up.

And the Greek disappears.

This wonderful joke dances on the edge of a terrible logical precipice. For while the Greek's love of eponymous deviant sexual practices is well-known, and the Italian's love of pizza certainly holds true to form, many listeners will experience a "gotcha" moment due to the non-disappearance of the Jew.

For surely, given the stereotypical Semitic love of money so nicely expressed by the act of reaching for a nickel, the Jew should have disappeared before the Greek.

But this reasoning is specious! The joke's logic is coherent! Saint Peter expressly states that "You have to refrain from doing your most favorite thing in the world." And, while the slavish pursuit of Mammon is indeed Chicken Soup to the Hebrew Soul, it does not rise to the vaunted level of "most favorite."

No, no. The favorite activity of the Jews is dancing around at midnight naked, sacrificing Christian babies while they sing terrible songs of praise to their savage and Ancient God before their ritual bath in the blood of innocents. Oh, how it would freeze your blood to stone if you had the misfortune to hear the half-human howls that they call hymns.

Thus, the Jew should not disappear. He is merely engaging in his second-favorite activity, scrounging for money.

Of course, since the Jew is not a goat, by all rights the Greek should remain present as well, but that pretty much ruins the punch line. Moreover, the Delta Lambda Phis are all remarkably gay, so the targeting of the Greek, Greek brother is superfluous.

WHAT WOMEN THINK IS FUNNY, BUT ISNT

This book is kind of geared toward a male reader. If you haven't noticed, it's because you're a guy. However, there is another side to the story. That's right, women think they have a sense of humor, too. Actually, some women are very funny. But that is generally born of intelligence, which means a guy like you probably won't get a chance to meet them.

—*Steve*

A couple is lying in bed. The man says, "I am going to make you the happiest woman in the world."

The woman says, "I'll miss you..."

* * * *

Jack says as he stepped out of the shower, "Honey, what do you think the neighbors would think if I mowed the lawn like this?"

"Probably that I married you for your money, "she replied.

* * * *

He said: Since I first laid eyes on you, I have wanted to make love to you really badly.

She said: Well, you succeeded.

* * * *

He said: Shall we try swapping positions tonight?

She said: That's a good idea . . . you stand by the ironing board while I sit on the sofa and fart.

* * * *

Q: What do you call an intelligent, good looking, sensitive man?

A: A rumor

* * * *

A man and his wife, now in their sixties, were celebrating their fortieth wedding anniversary. On their special day, a good fairy came to them and said that because they had been so good, each one of them could have one wish. The wife wished for a trip around the world with her husband. Whoosh! Immediately she had airline/cruise tickets in her hands.

The man wished for a female companion thirty years younger . . . Whoosh! . . . immediately he turned ninety!!!

A PRAYER....

Dear Lord,

I pray for Wisdom to understand my man; Love to forgive him; And Patience for his moods. Because, Lord, if I pray for strength, I'll beat him to death.

AMEN

* * * *

Q: How can you tell when a man is well hung?

A: When you can just barely slip your finger in between his neck and the noose.

* * * *

Q: Why do little boys whine?

A: They are practicing to be men.

* * * *

Q: How many men does it take to screw in a light bulb?

A: One-he just holds it up there and waits for the world to revolve around him.

OR Three — one to screw in the bulb, and two to listen to him brag about the screwing part.

* * * *

Q: What do you call a handcuffed man?

A: Trustworthy.

* * * *

Q: What does it mean when a man is in your bed gasping for breath and calling your name?

A: You did not hold the pillow down long enough.

* * * *

Q: Why does it take 100,000,000 sperm to fertilize one egg?
A: Because not one will stop and ask directions.

* * * *

Q: Why do female black widow spiders kill their males after mating?
A: To stop the snoring before it starts.

* * * *

Q: Why do men whistle when they are sitting on the toilet?
A: It helps them remember which end they need to wipe.

* * * *

Q: What is the difference between men and women?
A: A woman wants one man to satisfy her every need. A man wants every woman to satisfy his one need.

* * * *

Q: How do you keep your husband from reading your e-mail?
A: Rename the mail folder "Instruction Manuals"

* * * *

Once upon a time, there was a female brain cell who accidentally ended up in a man's head. She looked around nervously but it was all empty and quiet. "Hello?" she cried, but no answer. "Is there anyone here?" she cried a little louder, but still no answer. Now the female brain cell started to feel alone and scared and yelled at the top of her voice, "HELLO! IS THERE ANYONE HERE?" Then she heard a very faint voice from far, far away...
"We're down here!"

* * * *

Mick and Dave were sitting in a bar chatting when Mick mentions that he ran into John the other day.

"John," Dave says "I haven't seen John for ages. What's he doing with himself these days?"

Mick replies "He's gone back to the University, he's studying logic."

Dave is a bit confused "Logic??? What's logic?" So Mick explains what logic is. "You've got goldfish, right?"

"Yeah," says Dave.

"And you've got goldfish because you've got kids, right?"

"Yeah."

"And you've got kids because you're married?"

"That's right."

"And you're married because you're not gay?"

"Right again."

"Well," Mick says "That's logic."

Dave thinks about it and it all makes sense. Later that day Dave runs into Pete.

"Hi Pete."

"Hi Dave."

"Pete, I saw Mick earlier and he said he saw John a couple of days ago."

"I haven't seen John in months," Pete replies. "What's he up to?"

"Back at school," Dave says. "And he's studying logic."

"What's logic?" asks Pete.

"Well I'll explain it to you," says Dave. "You've got goldfish, right?"

"No," says Pete.

"Then you're gay."

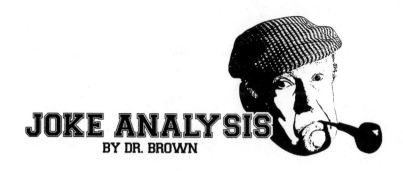

JOKE ANALYSIS
BY DR. BROWN

From the Goddess of Paganism to the persistent suffragette to the ladies in the house who say, "Yo-Oh" at the request of their favorite rapper, women have demanded a voice. Occasionally, this voice attempts to bend itself around humor. In terms of the joke form, this is not an intuitive exercise. I contend that there is a direct correlation between estrogen and comedy. They behave like vinegar and water; existing closely, but will never mixing.

This hypothesis is proven out by the following joke. It was not given to me by an *entire* woman, but by a pre-operative transsexual named Princess Mike. Clearly, his/her therapies had already begun to introduce enough estrogen to impair his/her joking ability.

Father O' Grady was saying his good-byes to the parishioners after a Sunday morning service as he always does when Mary Clancy came up to him in tears.

"What's bothering you, dear?" asked Father O' Grady.

"Oh, Father, I've got terrible news," replied Mary. "My husband passed away last night."

"Oh Mary!" said the father, "That's awful! Tell me Mary, did he have any last requests?"

"Yes..." Mary replied sheepishly.

"Well?" He said, "what was the last thing he said?"

Mary sighed . . . "He said, 'Please Mary, put the gun down.' "

Alas, while the punch line succeeds in giving the listener a pleasing "Switcheroonie," the joke more questions asked than answered.

Why are the main characters of this joke Irish? They don't drink. In direct contravention of every Irish joke ever told, not once is a reference made to the Hibernian's slavish devotion to alcoholic spirits. And, while the Irish are indeed known for their violent natures, theirs is a liquor-fueled fury more suited to fisticuffs than gunplay. If Princess Mike insists on making the woman Irish, then the punch line must be, "He said, 'Please Mary, put the shillelagh down.' "

JOKES THAT CAN BE MODIFIED TO BAG ON A SPECIFIC PERSON

Ever play "Madlibs?" This is the game in book form that tells stories but leaves blanks for words for the player to add, thus creating funny sentences, generally featuring the word "doody." Think of these jokes as short Madlibs that allow the teller to insert the name of a specific subject. They offer a wonderful opportunity to be simultaneously witty and cruel. And, if you're really lucky, you have a friend named Doody.

—*Steve*

One day after school _____ (female) told her mommy that the class did numbers today. She said the class went up to ten but she went all the way up to fifteen.

She then asked, "Am I able to do that because I'm a blonde mommy?"

Her mommy replied, "Yes honey. You're able to do that because you're a blonde."

The next day _____ (female) came home and told her, "Mommy, Mommy we did the alphabet today. The class went all the way up to F but I went all the way up to G. Am I able to do that because I'm a blond?" she asked.

Her mommy replied, "Yes, honey. You're able to do that because you're a blonde."

The very next day _____ (female) came home and said, "Mommy, we had gym class today and I noticed my boobies were bigger than all the other girls. Is that because I'm a blond she asked?"

Her mommy replied, "No honey. It's because you're nineteen years old."

* * * *

_____ (male) returns from Africa feeling very ill. He visits his doctor, who immediately rushes the guy to the intensive care unit at the local hospital. _____ (male) wakes up to the ringing of a telephone and answers it. "We've received the results from your tests," says the doctor on the other end of the line. "Bad news—you have Ebola."

"Oh, my God," cries the man. "Doc! What am I going to do?"

"Don't worry. First, we're going to put you on a diet of pizza, pancakes, and pita bread," says the doctor.

"Will that cure me?"

"No, but it's the only food we'll be able to get under the door."

* * * *

_____ (college professor) had just finished explaining an important research project to his class. He emphasized that this paper was an absolute requirement for passing his class, and that there would be only two acceptable excuses for being late. Those were a medically certifiable illness or a death in the student's immediate family. _____ (male) waved his hand and spoke up, "But what about extreme sexual exhaustion, Professor?"

As you would expect, the class exploded in laughter. When the students had finally settled down, the professor froze the young man with a glaring look.

"Well," he responded, "I guess you'll just have to learn to write with your other hand."

* * * *

_____ (female) walks into a pharmacy and tentatively approaches the pharmacist. The pharmacist, seeing her hesitancy, asks if there is anything that he can do for her. She asks him in a quiet voice, "Do you carry extra large condoms?" He points to where they are and asks if she wants to purchase a box. She says, "No, but do you mind if I wait here until someone does?"

* * * *

_____ (male) is walking along the shoreline at the beach. Sure enough he kicks up a bottle, pulls the cork, and out comes a genie to give him one wish. He pulls out a map of the Middle East and asks the genie if he can bring peace to this part of the world. The genie pales, and says, "Master, these people have been at war since time began. It is their nature, the very fiber of their lives. What you ask is totally impossible. It is probably the only wish I cannot grant you. Ask for anything else and I will make it happen."

"Okay," _____ (male) says, "tomorrow morning have _____ (subject's girlfriend) awaken me with the best blow job I've ever had, on her own, without my begging and pleading. Because SHE LIKES IT, because SHE WANTS TO, because IT TURNS HER ON!"

The genie shakes his head and says, "Let me see that map again."

* * * *

_____ (*uncircumcised male*) enters the hospital for a circumcision. When he comes to after the procedure, he's perturbed to see several doctors standing around his bed. "Son, there's been a bit of a mix-up," admits the surgeon. "I'm afraid there was an accident, and we were forced to perform a sex-change operation. You now have a vagina instead of a penis."

"What!" gasps _____ .

"You mean I'll never experience another erection?"

"Oh, you might," the surgeon reassures him. "Just not yours."

* * * *

_____ (*male*) says to his regular pimp, "This time send me a female with BIG TITS and a SMALL HOLE." Soon, a hooker arrives at the guy's house and asks, "Are you the guy with the big mouth and a small dick?"

* * * *

_____ (*male*) and _____ (*male 2 – preferably an idiot*) are out in the woods hunting when _____ (*male*) collapses. He doesn't seem to be breathing and his eyes are glazed. The other guy whips out his cell phone and calls the emergency services.

He gasps, "My friend is dead! What can I do?"

The operator says, "Calm down, I can help. First, let's make sure he's dead." There is a silence, and then a shot is heard.

Back on the phone, the guy says, "Okay, now what?"

* * * *

_____ (*male who lives with girlfriend*) was traveling through Nevada and stopped in a legal brothel. "I have $500. Give me a bologna sandwich and the ugliest girl you have," he told the madam.

"Honey," said the madam, "for $500 you can have a steak with all the trimmings and the belle of the ball!" "Oh, I'm not horny," explained _____ , "I'm homesick."

* * * *

_____ (male) is very upset and yells at his friend, "You slept with my wife, you son of a bitch. I am gonna make you pay for what you did."

"Bullshit," replies _____ (male 2). "Why should I pay twice."

* * * *

_____ (male) goes to pick up his date for the evening. She's not ready yet, so he has to sit in the living room with her parents. He has a bad case of gas and really needs to relieve some pressure. Then, the family dog jumps up on the couch next to him. He decides that he can let a little fart out and if anyone notices they will think that the dog did it. _____ (male) farts and the woman yells, "Spot, get down from there."

The guy thinks, "Great, they think the dog did it." He releases another fart, and the woman again yells for the dog to get down. This goes on for a couple more farts.

Finally the woman yells, "Dammit, Spot! Get down before he shits on you."

* * * *

One day _____ (male) came home early from work and was greeted by _____ (male's girlfriend) dressed in very sexy lingerie and heels. "Tie me up," she purred, "and you can do anything you want." So, he tied her up and played X-Box.

* * * *

_____ (male) moved into a new apartment, and went to the lobby to put his name on his mailbox. While he was there, an attractive young lady came out of the apartment next to the mailboxes wearing a robe.

_____ (male) smiled at the young woman and she started a conversation with him.

As they talked, her robe slipped open, and it was obvious that she had nothing else on. _____ (male) broke into a sweat trying to maintain eye contact. After a few minutes, she placed her hand on his arm and said, "Let's go to my apartment, I hear someone coming."

He followed her into her apartment; she closed the door and leaned against it, allowing her robe to fall off completely. Now nude, she purred at him, "What would you say is my best feature?"

Flustered and embarrassed, he finally squeaked, "It's got to be your ears!"

Astounded, and a little hurt she asked, "My ears? Look at these breasts; they are full and 100% natural! I work out every day! My butt is firm and solid! Look at my skin - no blemishes anywhere! How can you think that the best part of my body is my ears?"

Clearing his throat, he stammered, "Outside, when you said you heard someone coming? That was me."

* * * *

_____ (*male*) dies and goes straight to Hell. The devil greets him and immediately makes him face a big decision: "You may choose which room you wish to enter. Whichever room you choose, the person in that room will switch with you. They'll finally go to heaven after years of waiting and you'll take over until somebody switches with you. So go on, pick a room."

The devil leads him to the first room where someone is tied to a wall and is being whipped over and over again. In the second room is a man strapped to a table and being subjected to Chinese water torture. Finally, in the third room is a man sitting in a chair while being pleasured by a beautiful woman.

"I choose this room!" _____ (*male*) says.

"Very well," the devil says. He walks up to the woman and taps her on the shoulder.

You can go now. I've found your replacement."

* * * *

_____ (*A very flat-chested woman*) finally decided she needed a bra and set out to the mall in search of one in her size. She entered an upscale department store and approached the saleslady in lingerie,

"Do you have a size 28AAAA bra?"

The clerk haughtily replied in the negative, so she left the store and proceeded to another department store where she is rebuffed in much the same manner.

After a third try at another department store in the mall, she had become disgusted. Leaving the mall, she drove to K-Mart. Marching up to the sales clerk, she unbuttoned and threw open her blouse, yelling,

"Do you have anything for this?"

The lady looked closely at her and replied, "Have you tried Clearasil?"

* * * *

_____ (*male*) is very drunk. He walks out of a bar with a key in his hand and he is stumbling back and forth.

A cop on the beat sees him and approaches, "Can I help you, sir?"

"Yessh! Ssssomebody ssstole my carrr," the man replies.

The cop asks "Where was your car the last time you saw it?"

"It wasss on the end of thisshh key," the man replies.

About that time the cop looks down and sees the man's privates hanging out of his fly for the entire world to see.

He asks, "Sir, are you aware that you are exposing yourself?"

Momentarily confused, _____ (*male*) looks down at his crotch and, without missing a beat, blurts out "I'll be damned — My girlfriend's gone, too!"

* * * *

_____ (*male*) goes into a bar, orders twelve shots and starts drinking them as fast as he can.

The bartender says, "Dang, why are you drinking so fast?"

The guy says, "You would be drinking fast if you had what I had."

The bartender says, "What do you have?"

The guy says, "75 cents."

* * * *

_____ (*male*) is working as a bartender and while he's getting ready to close for the night, a robber bursts in and pulls a gun.

"This is a stickup!" He yells. "Put all your dough in a bag!"

"Don't shoot," pleads the barkeep. "I'll do whatever you say!"

The bartender stuffs all the money into a bag and hands it over. The crook snatches it and then puts the gun to the bartender's head and says, "All right, now give me a blow job!"

"Anything!" cries the bartender. "Just don't shoot!"

_____ (male) gets on his knees and starts blowing the guy. After a few minutes, the robber gets so excited he drops his gun.

The bartender picks the gun up off the floor and hands it back to the robber. "Hold the gun, dammit," he says. "One of my friends might walk in!"

* * * *

A guy was running for an elevator and he stuck his hand in to stop the doors, and the doors opened. Inside stood _____ (female). He said, "Good morning, which floor are you going to?"

She responded, "Third floor." He pushed the third floor button, plus the fifth floor for himself.

As the elevator started moving the gentleman struck up a conversation and asked _____ (female) where she was going.

She said, "I'm going to the blood bank on the third floor. I donate blood once a week for $10 to supplement my income." Then she asked the gentleman where he was going.

He responded, "I'm going to the sperm bank on the fifth floor. I donate sperm there once a week for $50 to supplement my income."

The next week the same scenario happens. He stopped the elevator doors with his hand, the doors opened and the blonde was standing inside. He smiled and greeted her and asked if she was going to the third floor.

_____ (female) responded in a garbled tone (as if she had something in her mouth), "No, fifth floor first."

* * * *

_____ (male) is approached by the lifeguard at the public swimming pool.

"You're not allowed to pee in the pool," said the lifeguard. "I'm going to report you."

"But everyone pees in the pool," said _____ (male).

"Maybe," said the lifeguard, "but not from the diving board!"

* * * *

_____ (male) met a girl at a nightclub and she invited him back to her place for the night. She still lived with her parents, but they were out of town, so this was the perfect opportunity.

They got back to her house, and they went into her bedroom. When _____ (male) walked in the door, he noticed all sorts of fluffy toys. There are hundreds of them; fluffy toys on top of the wardrobe, fluffy toys on the bookshelf and window sill. There are more on the floor, and of course fluffy toys all over the bed.

Later, after they've had sex, _____ (male) turned to her and asked, "So, how was I?"

She replied, "Well, you can take anything from the bottom shelf."

* * * *

Trying to disguise his voice, _____ (recently broken-up male) calls his ex and asks to speak to himself.

Jody, his ex, says, "_____ (recently broken-up male), look, we are not married anymore — quit bothering me !"

Next day, _____ (recently broken-up male) calls again, resulting in the same sequence of events.

The following day though when he called, his ex said, "Listen Bozo. I told you we're divorced, split, it's over — period! We're divorced. Why do you keep calling here?"

"I just love to hear you say it!"

* * * *

_____ (male) went to his buddy's fancy dress costume party with nothing but an inflatable, naked girl on his back.

"So what are you supposed to be?" the host asked indignantly.

"I'm a snail," _____ (male) replied.

The exasperated host asked, "How can you be a snail when all you've got is that naked girl on your back?"

_____ (male) replied. "That's Michelle."

* * * *

_____ (male) walks up and sits down at the bar. "What can I get you?" the bartender inquires.

"I want six shots of Jagermeister," responded _____ (male).

"6 shots? Are you celebrating something?"

"Yeah, my first blowjob."

"Well, in that case, let me give you a seventh on the house."

"No offense, but if 6 shots won't get rid of the taste, nothing will."

* * * *

_____ (male, preferably a small white guy) goes into an elevator. When he gets in, he notices a huge black dude standing next to him. The big black dude looks down upon _____ (male) and says, "7 foot tall, 350 pounds, 20 inch dick, 3 pound left ball, 3 pound right ball, Turner Brown."

_____ (male) faints!! The big black dude picks up the small white guy and brings him to, slapping his face and shaking him, and asks, "What's wrong?"

The small white guy says; "Excuse me but what did you say?"

The big black dude looks down and says "7 foot tall, 350 pounds, 20 inch dick, 3 pound left ball, 3 pound right ball, my name is Turner Brown."

_____ (male) says, "Thank god, I thought you said 'Turn around.' "

* * * *

A guy goes over to _____ (male's) house, rings the bell, and girlfriend _____ (female) answers. "Hi, is _____ (male) home?"

"No, he went to the store."

"Well, you mind if I wait?"

"No, come in."

They sit down and the _____ (male 2) says, "You know _____ (female), you have the greatest breasts I have ever seen. I'd give you a hundred bucks if I could just see one."

She thinks about this for a second and figures what the hell - a hundred bucks. She opens her robe and shows one. He promptly thanks her and throws a hundred bucks on the table. They sit there a while longer and _____ (male 2) says, "They are so beautiful I've got to see the both of them. I'll give you another hundred bucks if I could just see the both of them together."

_____ (female) thinks about this and thinks what the hell, opens her robe, and gives the guy a nice long look. He thanks her, throws another hundred bucks on the table, and then says he can't wait any longer and leaves.

A while later _____ (male) arrives home and _____ (female) tells him that his friend came over. _____ (male) thinks about this for a second, and says "Did he drop off the 200 bucks he owes me?"

JOKE ANALYSIS
BY DR. BROWN

Hey, _____ (*you*)! I'm too busy nailing _____ (*your mother's name*) to write this analysis.

By the way, did you know that _____ (*your father's name*) has no gag reflex? I didn't either, until _____ (*your fag brother*) told me.

JOKES EASY ENOUGH TO TELL WHILE DRUNK

There are those who have no problem being laughed at. Then there are those who would prefer to be laughed with. This selection of jokes is for those who would like to be laughed at right up until they're being laughed with. However, even if you can't get through them without a spitting out a bunch of burps, syrupy giggles and maybe even a vomiting spell, the laughs will still come. They are a win-win proposition!

—*Steve*

A man goes to a tattoo artist and says: "I'd like you to tattoo a one- hundred dollar bill onto my dick."

The tattoo artist is surprised: "Well, that could hurt a lot! Why would you want a 100 dollar bill on your dick?"

The man answers, "Three reasons: One: I like to watch my money grow. Two: I like to play with my money. And three: The next time my wife wants to blow a hundred bucks she won't have to leave the house!"

* * * *

On the first day of college, the chancellor addressed the students, pointing out some of the rules:

"The girl's dormitory will be out-of-bounds for all male students, and the guys dormitory to the female students. Anybody caught breaking this rule will be fined $50 the first time."

He continued, "Anybody caught breaking this rule the second time will be fined $100. Being caught a third time will cost you a fine of $300. Are there any questions?"

At this point, a male student in the crowd inquired: "How much for a semester pass?"

* * * *

A cowboy and his new bride ask the hotel desk clerk for a room. "Congratulations on your wedding!" the clerk says. "Would you like the bridal, then?"

"Naw, thanks," says the cowboy. "I'll just hold her by the ears till she gets the hang of it."

* * * *

An escaped convict breaks into a house and ties up the couple in the bedroom. As soon as he has a chance, the husband turns to his wife in the skimpy nightgown and says "Honey this guy hasn't seen a woman in years. Just do whatever he wants. If he wants to have sex, you just go along with it and pretend you like it. Our lives depend on it."

The wife whispers back, "Dear, I'm so relieved you feel that way, because that guy just whispered to me that you have a nice butt."

* * * *

After a long night of making love the young guy rolled over, pulled out a cigarette from his jeans and searched for his lighter. Unable to find it, he asked the girl if she had one at hand. "There might be some matches in the top drawer," she replied.

He opened the drawer of the bedside table and found a box of matches setting neatly on top of a framed picture of another man. Naturally, the guy began to worry. "Is this your husband?" he inquired nervously.

"No, silly," she replied, snuggling up to him.

"Your boyfriend then?" he asked.

"No, not at all," she said, nibbling away at his ear.

"Well, who is he then?" demanded the bewildered guy.

Calmly, the girl replied, "That's me before the operation."

* * * *

Two buddies are out drinking one night when one turns to the other and says, "You know, I don't know what else to do. Whenever I go home after we've been drinking, I turn the headlights off before I get into the driveway. I shut of the engine and coast into the garage. I take off my shoes before I go into the house, sneak upstairs. I get undressed in the bathroom. I ease into bed and my girlfriend *still* wakes up and yells at me for staying out so late."

His buddy looks at him and says, "We'll you're obviously taking the wrong approach. I screech into the driveway, slam the car door, storm up the steps, throw my shoes into the closet, jump into bed, slap her on the ass and say "Who's horny?" And she acts like she is sound asleep.

* * * *

Bubba died in a fire and his body was burned pretty badly. The morgue needed someone to identify the body, so they sent for his two best friends, Darryl and Gomer. The three men had always done everything together.

Darryl arrived first, and when the mortician pulled back the sheet, Darryl said, "Yup, his face is burned up pretty bad. You better roll him over." The mortician rolled him over, and Darryl said, "Nope, ain't Bubba."

The mortician thought this was rather strange. Then he brought Gomer in to identify the body. Gomer looked at the body and said, "Yup, he's pretty well burnt up. Roll him over." The mortician rolled him over and Gomer said, "No, it ain't Bubba."

The mortician asked, "How can you tell?"

Gomer said, "Well, Bubba had two assholes."

"What? He had two assholes?" asked the mortician.

"Yup, I've never seen 'em, but everyone knew he had two assholes. Every time we went to town, folks would say, 'Here comes Bubba with them two assholes.'"

* * * *

A pirate walked into a bar and the bartender said, "Hey, haven't seen you in a while. What happened? You look terrible."

"What do you mean?" said the pirate. "I feel fine."

"What about the wooden leg? You didn't have that before."

"Well, we were in a battle and I got hit with a cannon ball, but I'm fine now."

"Well, OK, but what about that hook? What happened to your hand?"

"We were in another battle. I boarded a ship and got into a sword fight. My hand was cut off. I got fitted with a hook. I'm fine, really."

"What about that eye patch?"

"Oh, one day we were at sea, and a flock of birds flew over. I looked up and one of them shit in my eye."

"You're kidding," said the bartender, "you couldn't lose an eye just from bird shit."

"It was my first day with the hook!"

* * * *

A drunken man staggers into a Catholic church and sits down in a confession box and says nothing. The bewildered priest coughs to attract his attention, but still the man says nothing. The priest then knocks on the wall three times in a final attempt to get the man to speak. Finally, the drunk replies, "No use knockin' dude. There's no paper in this one either."

****

Two guys, Bubba and Earl, were driving down the road drinking a couple of bottles of Bud. The passenger, Bubba, said, "Lookey thar up ahead, Earl, it's a police roadblock!! We're gonna get busted fer drinkin' these here beers!!"

"Don't worry, Bubba," Earl said. "We'll just pull over and finish drinkin' these beers then peel off the label and stick it on our foreheads, and throw the bottles under the seat."

"What fer?" asked Bubba.

"Just let me do the talkin', okay?" said Earl.

Well, they finished their beers, threw the empties out of sight and put label on each of their foreheads. When they reached the roadblock, the sheriff said, "You boys been drinkin'?"

"No, sir," said Earl while pointing at the labels. "We're on the patch."

****

A guy walks into a pool hall with his pet monkey. As he racks the balls, the monkey starts jumping all over the place. The monkey grabs some olives off the bar and eats them, then grabs some sliced limes and eats them, then jumps up on the pool table, grabs the cue ball, sticks it in his mouth, and swallows it whole.

The bartender screams at the guy, "Did you see what your monkey just did?"

The guy says, "No, what?"

"He just ate the cue ball off my pool table - whole!" says the bartender.

"Yeah, that doesn't surprise me," replies the patron. "He eats everything in sight, the little twerp. I'll pay for the cue ball and stuff." He finishes his drink, pays his bill, and leaves.

Two weeks later he's in the bar again, and he has his monkey with him. He orders a drink, and the monkey starts running around the bar again. While the man is drinking, the monkey finds a maraschino cherry on the bar. He grabs it, sticks it up his butt, pulls it out, and eats it.

The bartender is disgusted. "Did you see what your monkey did now?"

"Now what?" asks the patron.

"Well, he stuck a maraschino cherry up his butt, then pulled it out and ate it!" says the barkeeper.

"Yeah, that doesn't surprise me," replies the patron. "He still eats everything in sight, but ever since he ate that damn cue ball, he measures everything first!"

* * * *

A man from Texas buys a round of drinks for everyone in the bar as he announces his wife has just produced "A typical Texas baby boy weighing twenty pounds."

Congratulations shower all around, and many exclamations of 'wow!' are heard. Two weeks later he returns to the bar. The bartender says, "Say, you're the father of the typical Texas baby that weighed twenty pounds at birth, aren't you? How much does the baby weigh now?"

The proud father answers, "Fifteen pounds."

The bartender is puzzled. "Why? What happened? He already weighed twenty pounds at birth."

The Texas father takes a slow sip from his beer, wipes his lips on his shirt sleeve, leans over to the bartender and proudly announces, "Had him circumcised."

* * * *

Patrick, who was vacationing in the Bahamas couldn't seem to make it with any of the girls. So he asked the local lifeguard for some advice. "Mate, it's obvious," says the lifeguard, "you're wearing them old baggy swimming trunks that make ya look like an old geezer. They're years outta style. Your best bet is to grab yourself a pair of Speedos, about two sizes too small, and drop a fist-sized potato down inside 'em. I'm tellin' ya man... you'll have all the babes ya want!"

The following weekend, Patrick hits the beach with his spanking new tight Speedo, and his fist-sized potato. Everybody on the beach was disgusted as he walked by, covering their faces, turning away, laughing, looking sick! So he went back to the lifeguard again and asked him, "What's wrong now?"

"Damn, mate!" said the lifeguard, "The potato goes in front!!"

* * * *

There are two statues in a park, one of a nude man and one of a nude woman. They had been facing each other across a pathway for a hundred years, when one day an angel comes down from the sky and, with a single gesture, brings the two to life.

The angel tells them, "As a reward for being so patient through a hundred blazing summers and dismal winters, you have been given life for thirty minutes to do what you've wished to do the most."

He looks at her, she looks at him, and they go running behind the shrubbery.

The angel waits patiently as the bushes rustle and giggling ensues. After fifteen minutes, the two return, out of breath and laughing. The angel tells them, "Um, you have fifteen minutes left. Would you care to do it again?"

He asks her. "Shall we?"

She eagerly replies, "Oh, yes, let's! But let's change positions. This time, I'll hold the pigeon down, and you shit on its head."

* * * *

How do you make 5 pounds of fat look beautiful?
Put a nipple on it!

* * * *

A young girl goes for a haircut while eating a snack cake. During the haircut, the hair cutter warns, "You're getting hair on your Twinkie."

"Yeah," the girl replies, "and my tits are growing, too!"

* * * *

A man is at the bar, really drunk. Some guys decide to be good samaritans and get him home. They pick him up off the floor, and drag him out the door. On the way to the car, he falls down three times. When they get to his house, they help him out of the car, and he falls down five more times.

They ring the bell, and one says, "Here's your husband!"

The man's wife says, "Where the hell is his wheelchair?"

* * * *

One day mom was cleaning junior's room and in the closet she found a bondage S&M magazine. This was very upsetting for her. She hid the magazine until his father got home and showed it to him. He looked at it and handed it back to her without a word. She finally asked him, "Well what should we do about this?"

Dad looked at her and said, "Well I don't think you should spank him."

* * * *

A Chinese couple get married . . . and she's a virgin. Truth be told, he is not too experienced either.

On the wedding night, she cowers naked under the sheets as her husband undresses. He climbs in next to her and tries to be reassuring, "My darring. I know dis you firss time and you berry frighten. I pomise you, I give you anyting you want, I do anyting . . . juss anyting you want. Whatchou want?" he says, trying to sound experienced, which he hopes will impress his virgin bride.

A thoughtful silence follows and he waits patiently (and eagerly) for her request. She eventually replies shyly and unsure, "I wan try somethin I have heard bout. Numbaa 69."

More thoughtful silence, this time from him.

Eventually, in a puzzled tone he queries, "You want...Beef wiff Broccori?"

* * * *

Two casino dealers are at the craps table when a cute blonde comes over and says, "I want to bet twenty thousand dollars on a single roll of the dice. But, if you don't mind, I'd I feel much luckier if I were completely nude."

They say fine. She strips naked from the neck down, and rolls the dice. Then she screams, "I won! I won!"

She starts jumping up and down, hugs each of the dealers, and then picks up her money and her clothes and walks away. For a minute, the two dealers stare at each other.

Then the first one says, "What did she roll, anyway?"

The second dealer says, "I don't know. I thought you were watching."

* * * *

A mother walks into her daughter's room holding a condom in her hand, "I found this while cleaning your room today. Are you sexually active?"

To which the daughter replies, "No, I just lay there."

* * * *

A biology teacher was giving a lesson on the circulation of blood. Trying to make the matter clearer, he said: "Now, students, if I stood on my head, the blood, as you know, would run into it, and I should turn red in the face."

"Yes, sir," the students said.

"Then why is it that while I am standing upright in the ordinary position the blood doesn't run into my feet?"

Someone shouted, "It's because your feet aren't empty!"

* * * *

A guy is outside in his front yard attempting to fly a kite with his son. Every time the kite gets up in the air, it comes crashing back down. After a while, the guy's wife sticks her head out of the door and yells "You need more tail."

The guy turns to his son and says "Son, I will never understand women. I told her an hour ago I need more tail and she told me to go fly a kite."

* * * *

Bubba and Homer were sitting in back of their trailers, shooting the breeze. Bubba asked Homer, "If I snuck ovah to yore house while you wuz out fishin' an' I made love to yore wife, an' she got pregnant, would that make us kin?"

Homer scratched his head for a bit then said, "I don't think so, but it shore would make us even."

* * * *

A young couple with a box of condoms proceeded to burn some rubber. When they were finished, she discovered that there were only six condoms remaining in the box of twelve, so she asked him, "What happened to the other five condoms?"

His nervous reply was, "Er, I masturbated with them." Later, she then approached her male confidant friend, told him the story, and then asked him, "Have you ever done that?"

"Yeah, once or twice," he told her.

"You mean you've actually masturbated with a condom before?" she asked.

"Oh," he said, "I thought you were asking if I'd ever lied to my girlfriend."

* * * *

A man enters his bathroom as his wife is standing before the mirror, examining her breasts. "I wish they were bigger," she complains.

He's heard this before, and is tired of telling her they are just fine, so instead he says, "A good way to make them grow is to rub a piece of toilet paper between them for a few seconds every day." Desperate to try anything, she takes a piece of toilet paper and starts rubbing it between her breasts. "How long will this take?" she asks her husband. "A few years, maybe."

"Why do you think rubbing a piece of toilet paper between my breasts every day will make my breasts grow over the years?"

"It worked for your ass, didn't it?"

JOKE ANALYSIS
BY DR. BROWN

Some people drink to forget. Some, however, are so bereft of thought that the only thing they have in their minds to forget is where they put their drink. Such was the case with a young Spanish exchange student who referred to himself as Arturo Caliente. He was convinced he would be a masterful bull fighter because "Bulls can't jab for shit." He attempted to further impress with his advanced intelligence by sharing this joke. Apparently bulls aren't the only things he likes to butcher.

The mythical Greek gods and friends threw a helluva party. It went on day and night with much drinking, carousing, and coupling. The next morning, the god Thor awoke much the worse for wear. He felt terrible. He was still in bed when a stunning young goddess walked in. He didn't remember her from the party but manfully got up to introduce himself.

"Hello, I am Mighty Thor" he says.

She says "You're mighty Thor? I'm tho thor I can hardly pith!

You don't have to be an over-muscled Minnesota dairy farmer named Sven to know that Thor is a Nordic God worshipped by the Vikings. Yet Mr. Caliente blithely insinuates that Thor is a mythical Greek God as if it makes no difference to the joke. But if Thor were Greek, the correct punchline to this joke would be: "I'm tho thore I can hardly shit!"

FRIEND READY TO YAK? THESE JOKES SHOULD TAKE HIM ALL THE WAY

What is it about vomiting that Hollywood executives love? Have you ever noticed just how much puking takes place on screen? To make matters worse, I'm one of those people for whom watching vomiting is a perfect way to educe vomiting! In fact, even the protracted discussion of the subject of vomiting makes me sick. Seriously, first the gurgle, then the gagging cough, then the splash as the half-digested goop breaks like a thick wave into the porcelain . . . *oh shit . . !*

—*Steve*

A husband, one bright sunny morning, turns to his lovely wife, "Wife, we're going fishing this weekend, you, me and the dog."

The wife grimaces, "But I don't like fishing!"

"Look! We're going fishing and that's final."

"Do I have to go fishing with you . . . I really don't want to go!"

"Right. I'll give you three choices . . . One: You come fishing with me and the dog. Two: You give me a blow job. Three: You take it up the ass!"

The wife grimaces again, "But I don't want to do any of those things!"

"Wife, I've given you three options. You'll have to do one of them! I'm going to the garage to sort out my fishing tackle. When I come back, I expect you to have made up your mind!"

The wife thinks about it. Twenty minutes later, her husband comes back. "Well! What have you decided? Fishing with me and the dog, blow job, or ass?"

The wife complains some more and finally makes up her mind, "Okay, I'll give you a blow job!"

"Great!" He says and drops his pants. The wife is on her knees doing the business. Suddenly she stops, looks up at her husband, "Oh! It tastes absolutely disgusting. It tastes all shitty!"

"Yeah," says her husband "The dog didn't want to go fishing either."

* * * *

A drunk in a bar pukes all over his own shirt, which was brand new before he came in. "Damn, he says. "I puked on my shirt again. If the wife finds out, she's gonna kill me."

"Not to worry," says the bartender as he sticks a $20 bill in the drunk's pocket. "Just tell her someone puked on you and gave you some cash to cover the cleaning bill."

So the drunk goes home and tells his wife about the guy who puked on him. She reaches into his pocket and finds two twenties. "Why are there two twenties?" she asks.

The drunk replies, "Oh, yeah, he crapped in my pants, too."

* * * *

There was this couple who had been married for fifty years. They were sitting at the breakfast table one morning when the old gentleman said to his wife, "Just think, honey, we've been married for fifty years."

"Yeah," she replied, "Just think, fifty years ago we were sitting here at this breakfast table together."

"I know," the old man said, "We were probably sitting here naked as jaybirds fifty years ago."

"Well," Granny snickered, "What do you say . . . should we get naked?" Where upon the two stripped to the buff and sat down at the table.

"You know, honey," the little old lady breathlessly replied, "my nipples are as hot for you today as they were fifty years ago."

"I wouldn't be surprised," replied Gramps. "One's in your coffee and the other is in your oatmeal."

* * * *

A guy walks into a liquor store and tells the clerk to get him a case of beer. Anything but Stroh's. The clerk fills his request, but curiosity gets the best of him and he asks the guy what he has against Stroh's.

The guy responds, "Last night, I drank a case of Stroh's and blew chunks."

"Anyone who drinks that much beer in one sitting is bound to throw up," the clerk responds.

"No you don't understand," the guy answers, "Chunks is my dog!"

* * * *

A policeman is on scene at a terrible accident . . . body parts everywhere. He is making his notes of where the pieces are and comes across a head.

He writes in his notebook: "Head on bullevard" and scratches out his error.

"Head on bouelevard" Nope, doesn't look right - scratch scratch.

"Head on boolevard..." dang it! Scratch scratch.

He looks around and sees that no one is looking at him as he kicks the head.

"Head on curb."

* * * *

Two cannibals are eating a clown. One says to the other: "Does this taste funny to you?"

* * * *

A man woke up every morning and passed gas. After about eight or nine years of marriage, his wife finally said, "If you fart any more, you'll fart your guts out." Her husband grunted in the usual way, ignored the comment, and kept on farting.

Being a butcher, his cunning wife decided to put pig scraps in his pants so he would wake up, and not do it anymore.

He woke up in the morning and went across the hall to the bathroom. After two long hours , he came out and stated, "Honey, you were right about me farting my guts out. But with the grace of the dear lord and these two fingers, I got them back in there!"

* * * *

Two men are sitting around drinking. One guys says to the other, "I bet I could gross you out right now"

The other guy says, "No way you could gross me out. Whatever you do, I could top." So the first guy looks at the second guy and sticks his fingers down his throat and vomits all over the table.

The second guy looks at him and says "Nice try," and pulls out a straw . . .

* * * *

Bob goes into the public restroom and sees this guy standing next to the urinal. The guy has no arms. As Bob's standing there, taking care of business, he wonders to himself how the poor wretch is going to take a leak.

Bob finishes and starts to leave when the man asks Bob to help him out. Being a kind soul, Bob says, "Ah, okay, sure, I'll help you."

The man asks, "Can you unzip my zipper?"

Bob says, "Okay."

Then the man says, "Can you pull it out for me?"

Bob replies, "Uh, yeah, okay."

Bob pulls it out and it has all kinds of mold and red bumps, with hair clumps, rashes, moles, scabs, scars, and reeks something awful. Then the guy asks Bob to point it for him, and Bob points for him. Bob then shakes it, puts it back in and zips it up.

The guy tells Bob, "Thanks, man, I really appreciate it."

Bob says, "No problem, but what the hell's wrong with your penis?"

The guy pulls his arms out of his shirt and says, "I don't know, but I ain't touching it."

* * * *

An extremely modest man was in the hospital for a series of tests, the last of which had left his system upset. Upon making several false-alarm trips to the bathroom he decided the latest was another and stayed put. He suddenly filled his bed with diarrhea and was embarrassed beyond his ability to remain rational.

Losing his presence of mind, he jumped up, gathered up the bed sheets, and threw them out the hospital window. A drunk was walking by the hospital when the sheets landed on him. He started yelling, cursing, and swinging his arms wildly, which left the soiled sheets in a tangled pile at his feet.

As the drunk stood there staring down at the sheets, a security guard who had watched the whole incident walked up and asked, "What the hell happened?"

Still staring down, the drunk replied: "I think I just beat the shit out of a ghost!"

* * * *

Q: What's the worst thing about a lung transplant?

A: Coughing up someone else's phlegm.

* * * *

Three whores decide to see who has the biggest snatch. They get naked, and start fingering themselves and each other.

After a few minutes, the first one squats on a glass top table, and then they measure the slimy outline she leaves.

The second one then squats on the table, and then they measure the slimy outline she leaves, which is even bigger.

The third one squats on the table, but when she stands back up, the first whore says, "You didn't leave an outline."

She says, "Smell the rim."

* * * *

A kid goes up to his father and says, "Hey, Pop, know how old I am today?"

His father says, "No . . . how old?"

He says, "I'm eleven!"

He goes into the kitchen and says to his grandmother, "Hey, Grandma, know how old I am today?"

She says, "Come closer . . ."

She unzips his jeans and reaches her thin, spotted arm down into his underwear.

She fondles his genitals for a few minutes and then she says, "You're eleven."

He says, "How could you tell?"

She says, "I heard you tell your father."

* * * *

A man walks into a pub and sits down at a table. He notices a leper at the bar. He orders a shot, drinks the shot and then throws up. Next he orders a beer, drinks the beer and then throws up. He does this for several more drinks when finally the leper comes over to his table and asks him, "I'm sorry if my appearance is making you ill."

And the man replies, "No, it's not you. It's the man next to you dipping his chips into your neck."

* * * *

A man and his newlywed check into a mountain resort by a lake. The desk clerk notices the "Just Married" sign still on the car. As soon as the man gets the luggage out of the car, he hops in a boat to go fishing.

He is out all day, comes back for a quick supper, picks up his lantern and goes back out at night. This goes on for a couple of days when the man happens to stop by the desk. The clerk starts a conversation with the man and mentions his behavior.

"I know it's none of my business, but I was wondering why you weren't having sex with your new wife."

"Oh, I couldn't do that; she has gonorrhea."

"Well, what about anal sex?"

"Couldn't do that; she has diarrhea."

"There is always oral sex."

"Nope, she has pyorrhea."

"Wait a second. If she has gonorrhea, diarrhea, and pyorrhea, why did you marry her?"

"That's easy. She also has worms, and I love to fish!"

JOKE ANALYSIS
BY DR. BROWN

Sometimes the most offensive act within a joke scenario is not so obvious. Factors widely considered "gross" are, indeed, the more acceptable to the senses than peripheral activities that are arguably less heinous. Such is the case in this joke, which was offered to me by "Mittens," a high-dive champion from an Ivy League university who was forced to act as my maid after running her uninsured vehicle into my cello.

A man was charged with having sex with a goat. The man didn't have enough money to hire the best lawyer in town, so he hired another lawyer who was famous for picking a sympathetic jury.

During the trial, the next door neighbor was recounting how she saw her neighbor having relations with the goat under the light of a full moon. She recounted that when the man had finished, the goat turned around and gave the man a big kiss right on the mouth.

At this testimony, the man and his lawyer turned to look at the jury to see their reaction. Just at that moment, one of the jurors turned to one of the other jurors and said, "A good goat will do that."

Quite possibly from personal experience, this joke reveals a profound understanding of the Criminal Justice system and the importance of Jury Selection, or Voir Dire, on the outcome of a trial.

And yet, something is not quite right with his story.

Given that in a criminal trial, lawyers have a number of peremptory challenges which may be exercised arbitrarily and without explanation, it is theoretically conceivable that a jury of goatfuckers could be picked.

But how?

The obvious response is "pick all Scotsmen."

But that suffers from a number of difficulties. Firstly, many Scotsmen frown upon relations with goats, feeling it a terrible sin to have sex with anything that's neither woman nor sheep.

More importantly, by law, peremptory challenges may never be exercised in a discriminatory manner. While this is usually almost impossible to prove, nonetheless, even the most tolerant judge will look very closely at a jury consisting of 12 angry men in kilts.

To judges, trained as they are to keep a keen eye for any procedural irregularities, the sound of bagpipes drifting in from the Jury break room serves as a red flag. Such blatant rigging will rarely be permitted.

Yet if ethnic homogeneity is impossible, what other groups could an attorney blend in with a healthy dose of Scotsmen? Greeks? Certainly. Serbs? Yes. Bosnians? Undoubtedly. Arabs? Only if there are no camels available.

But once again, such a jury pool poses problems. For to be totally accurate, the joke would have to be rewritten as follows:

. . . At this testimony, the man and his lawyer turned to look at the jury to see their reaction. Just at that moment, Balkan hatred bubbled over, and the Serbian juror began throttling his Bosnian compatriot. The Arab juror continued playing on his Microsoft Flight Simulator, and the Greek juror turned to the Scotsman and said, "Heh, heh, A good goat will do that." To which the Scotsman replied, "Oy, shut your gob, you pasty-faced boy-lover! I'm trying to listen to the dirty stories!"

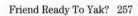

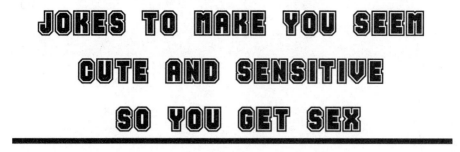

JOKES TO MAKE YOU SEEM CUTE AND SENSITIVE SO YOU GET SEX

You know what you are, little man? You're frisky. Yes, frisky and mischievous with a little bad thrown in for good measure. How could a girl resist a playful little Puck like you? She totally couldn't. See we're I'm going with this? These naughty little stories should have your dream date eating right out of your lap.

—Steve

Little Johnny was sitting in class doing math problems when his teacher picked him to answer a question.

"Johnny, if there were five birds sitting on a fence and you shot one with your gun, how many would be left?"

"None," replied Johnny, "'cause the rest would fly away."

"Well, the answer is four," said the teacher, "but I like the way you're thinking."

Little Johnny says, "I have a question for you. If there were three women eating ice cream cones in a shop, one was licking her cone, the second was biting her cone, & the third was sucking her cone, which one is married?"

"Well," said the teacher nervously, "I guess the one sucking the cone."

"No," said Little Johnny, "the one with the wedding ring on her finger, but I like the way you're thinking."

* * * *

Susan was in her late thirties and still not married. She just had a hard time meeting men. And the men she did meet all ended up being jerks. Finally, she decided to place an ad in the personals section of the newspaper. She wrote: "Looking for a man who won't beat me, won't leave me, and is excellent in bed."

Several days went by and she hadn't gotten a single call. Then one day, she was doing her laundry when she heard a knock on the door. She walked upstairs to answer it. She opened the door and saw a man in a wheelchair with no arms and no legs. "Can I help you?" she asked. He said, "I am the man of your dreams!"

She was baffled. She said, "Excuse me?"

"I read your personal ad in the paper and I am the perfect man for you. I have no arms, so I can't beat you. I have no legs, so I can never leave you."

"But are you good in bed?" she asked.

He replied, "How do you think I knocked on the door?!"

* * * *

Dr. Calvin Rickson, a scientist from Texas A&M University has invented a bra that keeps women's breasts from jiggling and prevents the nipples from pushing through the fabric when cold weather sets in.

At a news conference, after announcing the invention, a large group of men took Dr. Rickson outside and kicked the shit out of him.

* * * *

At an art exhibition, a couple was viewing a painting of three very naked and very black men sitting on a park bench. What was unusual was that the men on the ends of the bench had black penises, but the man in the middle had a very pink penis. While the couple was scratching their heads trying to figure this out, the artist walked by and noticed the couple's confusion. "Can I help you with this painting?" he asked.

"Well, yes" said the gentleman. We were curious about this picture of the black men on the bench. Why is it that the man in the middle has a pink penis?"

"Oh" said the artist. "I'm afraid you've misunderstood the painting. The three men are not Africans, they're coal miners, and the fellow in the middle went home for lunch."

* * * *

There was a guy who was struggling to decide what to wear to go to a fancy costume party. Then he had a bright idea. When the host answered the door, he found the guy standing there with no shirt and no socks on. "What the hell are you supposed to be?" asked the host.

"A premature ejaculation, " said the man. "I just came in my pants!"

* * * *

Jill and Nadine get together for lunch. "You're looking very tired today, Nadine. Did you have a late night?" asks Jill.

"Yes," replied Nadine, "but it was all very strange. While doing some gardening yesterday, I found a lamp, so I rubbed it and out popped a genie. He gave me a choice of two wishes."

"Wow," says Jill, "so what were the choices he gave you, Nadine?"

"He said he could either give me an excellent, sharp, 100% memory or else he could give my boyfriend a bigger penis."

"So tell me, what did you choose?"

"I can't remember."

* * * *

A father passing by his college student son's bedroom was astonished to see the bed was nicely made and everything was picked up. Then he saw an envelope propped up prominently on the center of the bed. It was addressed, "Dad." With the worst premonition, he opened the envelope and read the letter with trembling hands.

Dear Dad,

It is with great regret and sorrow that I'm writing this. I had to elope with my new girlfriend because i wanted to avoid a scene with mom and you. I've been finding real passion with Barbara and she is so nice, even with all her piercings, tattoos, and her tight motorcycle clothes. But it's not only the passion, Dad, she's pregnant and Barbara said that we will be very happy.

Even though you don't care for her as she is much older than I, she already owns a shack in the woods and has a stack of firewood for the whole winter. She wants to have many more children with me and that's now one of my dreams too.

Barbara taught me that marijuana doesn't really hurt anyone and we'll be growing it for ourselves and trading it with her friends for all the cocaine and ecstasy we want. In the meantime, we'll pray that science will find a cure for AIDS so Barbara can get better. She sure deserves it!!

Don't worry Dad, I'm 17 years old now and i know how to take care of myself. Someday I'm sure we'll be back to visit so you can get to know your grandchildren.

Your son, John

p.s. Dad, none of this is true. I'm over at the neighbor's house. I just wanted to remind you that there are worse things in life than my report card that's in my desk, center drawer.

* * * *

My housework-challenged roommate decided one day that he wanted to wash his favorite sweatshirt.

As he entered the laundry room, he yelled, "What setting do I put the washer on?"

I shouted back, "What does it say on your shirt?"

His reply was, "University of Arizona!"

* * * *

Two deaf people get married. During the first week of marriage, they find that they are unable to communicate in the bedroom when they turn off the lights because they can't see each other using sign language. After several nights of fumbling around and misunderstandings, the wife decides to find a solution. "Honey," she signs, "Why don't we agree on some simple signals? For instance, at night, if you want to have sex with me, reach over and squeeze my left breast one time. If you don't want to have sex, reach over and squeeze my right breast one time."

The husband thinks this is a great idea and signs back to his wife, "Great idea! Now, if you want to have sex with me, reach over and pull on my penis one time. If you don't want to have sex, reach over and pull on my penis fifty times."

* * * *

It's the spring in 1957 and Bobby goes to pick up his date. He's a pretty hip guy with his own car. When he goes to the front door, the girl's father answers and invites him in. "Carrie's not ready yet, so why don't you have a seat?" He says.

"That's cool," says Bobby. Carrie's father asks Bobby what they're planning to do. Bobby replies politely that they will probably just go to the soda shop or a movie.

Carrie's father responds, "Why don't you two go out and screw? I hear all the kids are doing it."

Naturally, this comes as quite a surprise to Bobby, so he asks Carrie's dad to repeat it.

"Yeah," says Carrie's father, "Carrie really likes to screw. She'll screw all night if we let her!"

Well, this just made Bobby's eyes light up, and his plan for the evening was beginning to look pretty good.

A few minutes later, Carrie comes downstairs in her little poodle skirt and announces that she's ready to go.

Almost breathless with anticipation, Bobby escorts his date out the front door.

About twenty minutes later, Carrie rushes back into the house, slams the door behind her, and screams at her father, "For God's sake Dad! It's called the Twist!"

* * * *

A young man at this construction site was bragging that he could outdo anyone based on his strength. He especially made fun of one of the older workman. After several minutes, the older worker had enough.

"Why don't you put your money where you mouth is?" he said. "I'll bet a week's wages that I can haul something in a wheelbarrow over to the other building that you won't be able to wheel back."

"You're on, old man," the young man replied. "Let's see what you've got."

The old man reached out and grabbed the wheelbarrow by the handles. Then nodding to the young man, he said with a smile,

"All right. Get in."

* * * *

The other night I was invited out for a night with "the girls." I told my husband that I would be home by midnight, "I promise!" Well, the hours passed and the margaritas went down way too easy. Around 3 AM, a bit the worse for wear, I headed for home.

Just as I got in the door, the cuckoo clock in the hall started up and cuckooed three times. Quickly, realizing my husband would probably wake up, I cuckooed another nine times. I was really proud of myself for coming up with such a quick-witted solution, in order to escape a possible conflict with him. (Even when totally smashed . . . 3 cuckoos plus 9 cuckoos totals 12 cuckoos=midnight!)

The next morning my husband asked me what time I got in, and I told him "Midnight". He didn't seem cross at all. Whew! Got away with that one! Then he said, "We need a new cuckoo clock."

When I asked him why, he said, "Well, last night our clock cuckooed three times, then said, 'Oh shit,' cuckooed four more times, cleared its throat, cuckooed another three times, giggled, cuckooed twice more, and then tripped over the coffee table and farted."

* * * *

During class, a teacher trying to teach good manners asks the students, one by one "Michael, if you were on a date, having supper with a nice young lady, how would you tell her that you have to go to the bathroom?" she asked.

"Just a minute, I have to go piss."

The teacher replied "That would be rude and impolite!"

"What about you John, how would you say it?"

"I am sorry, but I really need to go to the bathroom, I'll be right back."

The teacher responded, "That's better, but it's still not very nice to say the word bathroom at the table."

"And you Peter, are you able to use your intelligence for once and show us your good manners?"

"I would say: Darling, may I please be excused for a moment, I have to shake hands with a very dear friend of mine, whom I hope you'll get to meet after supper."

* * * *

A man and a woman were having drinks when they got into an argument about who enjoyed sex more.

The man said, "Men obviously enjoy sex more than women. Why do you think we're so obsessed with getting laid?"

"That doesn't prove anything," the woman countered. "Think about this: When your ear itches and you put your little finger in it and wiggle it around, then pull it out, which feels better . . . your ear or your finger?"

* * * *

"I'm telling you, Jill, I've never been happier," Linda told her friend. "I have two boyfriends. One is just fabulous...handsome, sensitive, caring and considerate."

"What in the world do you need the second one for?" Jill asked.

"Oh,"Linda replied, "the second one is straight."

* * * *

An elderly woman went into the doctor's office. When the doctor asked why she was there, she replied, "I'd like to have some birth control pills."

Taken aback, the doctor thought for a minute and then said, "Excuse me, Mrs. Smith, but you're 72 years old. What possible use could you have for birth control pills?"

The woman responded, "They help me sleep better."

The doctor thought some more and continued, "How in the world do birth control pills help you to sleep?"

The woman said, "I put them in my college student granddaughter's orange juice every morning and I sleep better at night."

* * * *

Little Johnny was in his class when the teacher asked the children what their fathers did for a living. All the typical answers came up, fireman, policeman, salesman, and so on.

Johnny was being uncharacteristically quiet, and so the teacher asked him about his father. "My father's an exotic dancer in a gay cabaret and takes off all his clothes in front of other men. Sometimes, if an offer is really good, he'll go out to the alley with some guy and have sex with him for money."

The teacher, obviously shaken by this statement, hurriedly set the other children to work on some coloring, and took little Johnny aside to ask him, "Is that really true about your father?"

"No," said Johnny, "he's actually a lawyer, but I was too embarrassed to say so in front of the other kids!"

* * * *

How long a minute is depends on what side of the bathroom door you're on.

* * * *

Once upon a time there was a stork family - Papa stork, Mama stork and Baby stork. One evening, Papa stork didn't show up for dinner. Mama stork and Baby stork left the food out for him but he didn't come home at all that night. When Papa stork finally did come home the next day, Baby stork asked, "Papa stork, where were you last night?"

"Out making a young couple very happy,' replied Papa stork.

Several weeks later, Mama stork was late for dinner. Baby stork and Papa stork waited a while, and then gave up and ordered pizza. Mama stork didn't come home until late the next morning. When Mama stork did come in, Baby stork asked, "Mama stork, where were you last night?"

"Out making a young couple very happy," replied mama stork.

Later in the fall, Baby stork was late for dinner. Papa stork and Mama stork were worried. Their anxiety increased when Baby stork still wasn't home by sunset. They both waited up late for Baby stork but he didn't come in until early in the morning. His feathers were rumpled and unkempt. Papa stork barked, "Where the hell were you baby stork?' as his tired son dragged himself over the threshold.

"Out scaring the shit out of college students," replied baby stork.

* * * *

The kindergarten class had a homework assignment to find out about something exciting and relate it to the class the next day. When the time came for the little kids to give their reports, the teacher was calling on them one at a time. She was reluctant to call upon Little Johnny, knowing that he sometimes could be a bit crude. But eventually his turn came. Little Johnny walked up to the front of the class, and with a piece of chalk, made a small white dot on the blackboard, then sat back down. Well the teacher couldn't figure out what Johnny had in mind for his report on something exciting, so she asked him just what that was.

"It's a period," reported Johnny.

"Well I can see that," she said. "but what is so exciting about a period."

"Damned if I know," said Johnny, "but this morning, my sister called from college and said she missed one. Then Daddy had a heart attack, Mommy fainted and the man next door shot himself."

* * * *

The graduate with a Science degree asks, "Why does it work?"
The graduate with an Engineering degree asks, "How does it work?"
The graduate with an Accounting degree asks, "How much will it cost?"
The graduate with a Liberal Arts degree asks, "Do you want mustard with that?"

* * * *

It's a regular class at a university. Forum type, 300 to 400 students. The teacher is notoriously nasty with people who are tardy and he has a policy that when he says, "STOP," you stop taking your exam. Well one day he yells STOP! All the students stop and turn their tests in, except for one student. So the teacher thinks, "Okay, I'll let him keep going to waste his time."

So five minutes pass and the late student walks up and tries to turn in his paper. But the professor says, "I'm sorry, I can't take your paper."

"Why not?"

"Because you're late," replied the professor.

"Do you know who I am?" the student says angrily.

"No."

Raising his voice, the student snaps, "Do you know who I AM?"

The professor, acting nonchalantly, replies, "No."

So the student grabs the stacks of tests, shoves his tests in the middle of the pile and walks off.

* * * *

Nursery school teacher says to her class, "Who can use the word 'definitely' in a sentence?"

First a little girl says, "The sky is definitely blue."

Teacher says, "Sorry, Amy, but the sky can be gray, black, or orange."

A little boy raises his hand. "Trees are definitely green."

"Sorry, but in the autumn, the trees are brown."

Little Johnny from the back of the class stands up and asks, "Does a fart have lumps?"

The teacher looks horrified and says, "Johnny! Of course not!"

"Okay . . . then I DEFINITELY shit my pants!"

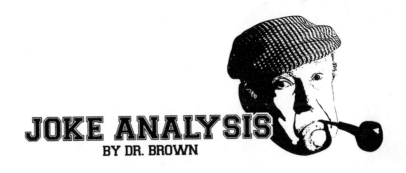

JOKE ANALYSIS
BY DR. BROWN

After a couple of solid laughs a woman might find even a Woody Allen attractive. But, you have to know when to stop. "I think you're funny" sex offers itself up like a bus; it stops at the corner for a moment and if you don't get on, you've missed it. Keep your jokes brief and or you can overplay your hand. This joke, the favored date joke of a first string quarterback for the Trojans, must have robbed him of a virtual freight car of cheerleader ass.

An ambitious yuppie finally decided to take a vacation. He booked himself on a Caribbean cruise and proceeded to have the time of his life . . . until the boat sank! The man found himself swept up on the shore of an island with no other people, no supplies. Nothing. Only bananas and coconuts.

After about four months, he is lying on the beach one day when the most gorgeous woman he has ever seen rows up to him. In disbelief he asks her:

"Where did you come from? How did you get here?"

"I rowed from the other side of the island," she says. "I landed here when my cruise ship sank."

"Amazing," he says. "You were really lucky to have a rowboat wash up with you."

"Oh, this?" replies the woman. "I made the rowboat out of raw material that I found on the island; the oars were whittled from gum tree branches; I wove the bottom from palm branches; and the sides and stern came from a Eucalyptus tree."

"But-but, that's impossible," stutters the man. "You had no tools or hardware. How did you manage?"

"Oh, that was no problem," replies the woman. "On the south side of the island, there is a very unusual strata of alluvial rock exposed. I found that if I fired it to a certain temperature in my kiln, it melted into forgeable ductile iron. I used that for tools and used the tools to make the hardware."

The guy is stunned. "Let's row over to my place, " she says.

After a few minutes of rowing, she docks the boat at a small wharf. As the man looks onto shore, he nearly falls out of the boat. Before him is a stone walk leading to an exquisite bungalow painted in blue and white.

While the woman ties up the rowboat with an expertly woven hemp rope, the man can only stare ahead, dumbstruck. As they walk into the house, her beautiful breasts bouncing with each step, she says casually, "It's not much, but I call it home. Sit down please; would you like to have a drink?"

"No thank you," he says, still dazed. "Can't take any more coconut juice."

"It's not coconut juice," the woman replies. "I have a still. How about a Pina Colada?"

Trying to hide his continued amazement, the man accepts, and they sit down on her couch to talk. After they have exchanged their stories, the woman announces, "I'm going to slip into something more comfortable. Would you like to take a shower and shave? There is a razor upstairs in the cabinet in the bathroom."

No longer questioning anything, the man goes into the bathroom. There, in the cabinet, is a razor made from a bone handle. Two shells honed to a hollow ground edge are fastened onto its end, inside of a swivel mechanism.

"This woman is amazing," he muses. "What next?"

When he returns, she greets him wearing nothing but vines and a shell necklace — strategically positioned — and smelling faintly of gardenias.

She beckons for him to sit down next to her. "Tell me," she begins suggestively, slithering closer to him, "we've been out here for a very long time. You've been lonely. I've been lonely. There's something I'm sure you really feel like doing right about now, something you've been longing for all these months? You know... " She stares into his eyes.

He can't believe what he's hearing. His heart begins to pound. He's truly in luck: "You mean . . ." he gasps, ". . . I can actually check my e-mail from here??"

Forget, if you can, that the joke relies on the untenable assumption that a woman could understand the principles of metallurgy, yet still desire sex with men. Sure, it's possible, but it's as likely as a man "scoring" at the Dinah Shore Classic LPGA event. Some quantum physicists have theorized that such an event could happen, but only under tightly controlled laboratory conditions involving Charlie Sheen, a cyclotron and a stick of butter.

Forget, if you can, that the joke posits a woman who can whittle canoes out of eucalyptus trees, yet is still unable to fashion even the most rudimentary wooden phallus to pleasure herself to satiety.

But, try as might, you will always remember how long this joke is. Not since itinerant Indian storytellers roamed the subcontinent subjecting unwary audiences to the 100,000 couplets of the Mahabharata have human beings been subjected to a tale of this length.

Does the "Can I check my e-mail" punchline warrant such a set-up? Of course not. It's as if all of Moby Dick were simply a 400 page prelude in order for Queequeg to say "Ah, I've seen whiter whales. You should have seen the whale I saw yesterday. Now THAT was a white whale!"

True, this joke relies on a classic bait and switch premise. A man turns out to hope for something other than sex with a beautiful woman. But, after several minutes of bait, even the dullest listener must become aware that he is becoming set up for a switch.

To truly surprise the listener, a daring joke-teller may be tempted to perform no switch at all and tell the punchline as follows:

He can't believe what he's hearing. His heart begins to pound. He's truly in luck: "You mean. . ." he gasps, ". . . I can actually turn you on your stomach and treat you like a cheap plastic fuck-doll with a vibrating anus?"

Unfortunately, this seemingly brilliant gambit only works if the intended audience is aware of the original joke. And let me assure the reader that no one who has heard this joke will stand still to hear it again. Far from it. The "fight or flight" response will take over, leaving the raconteur with a 50/50 chance of getting punched in the face, and no chance of getting a laugh.

Rather, the prospective comedian is best advised to go with a far shorter joke, such as this one:

Two fish are in a tank. One says to the other, "How do you drive this thing?"

RUDE, SEXIST JOKES TO GET HER OUT OF YOUR ROOM THE NEXT MORNING

Being handsome and charming is great . . . to a point. Trust me. Once you've beguiled your lady with snappy wit and mediocre mixology and had your way with her (whatever your "way" happens to be. Mine involves Sergio Mendez playing low, a pitcher of mai-tais and about two pints of liquid latex . . . and a kiddy sand shovel . . . and the blue sticker from the side of a banana . . . okay, I have very specific needs), eventually, you will have to get her gone. These jokes, if told properly, should offend her all the way back to Girlnextdoorfaceville.

—*Steve*

Q. What's the smartest thing ever to come out of a woman's mouth?
A. Albert Einstein's dick.

* * * *

A man wearing a bandanna bursts into a sperm bank with a shot gun. "Open the fucking safe!" he yells at the girl behind the counter.

"But we're not a real bank" replies the girl. "This is a sperm bank, we don't hold money."

"Don't argue just open the safe or I'll blow your fucking head off!" She obliges and opens the safe door. "Take one of the bottles and drink it!"

"But it's full of sperm," the girl replies nervously.

"Don't argue, just drink it" he says. She pries off the cap and gulps it down.

"Take out another one and drink it too!" he demands.

The girl drinks another one. Suddenly the guy pulls off the bandanna and to the girl's amazement it's her husband. "Not that fucking difficult is it?" he says.

* * * *

Q. Who makes more money? A drug dealer or a prostitute?
A. A prostitute because she can wash her crack and sell it again!

* * * *

Two hookers were standing on a street corner ready for a night of business. "It's gonna be a good night tonight, I can tell," says one of the girls.

"How can you tell?" says the other.

"I can smell cock in the air," replies the first hooker.

"Sorry," her friend replied, "I just burped!"

* * * *

The husband emerged from the bathroom naked and was climbing into bed when his wife complained, as usual, "I have a headache."

"Perfect," her husband said. "I was just in the bathroom powdering my dick with aspirin. You can take it orally or as a suppository, it's up to you!

* * * *

Q. Why are women like condoms?
A. They spend 90% of their time in your wallet and the remaining 10% on your dick!!!

* * * *

A man and his wife go to their honeymoon hotel for their 25th anniversary. As the couple reflected on that magical evening 25 years ago, the wife asked the husband, "When you first saw my naked body in front of you, what was going through your mind?"
The husband replied, "All I wanted to do was to fuck your brains out, and suck your tits dry."
Then, as the wife undressed, she asked, "What are you thinking now?"
He replied, "It looks as if I did a pretty good job."

* * * *

Q. Why is the area between a woman's tits and her ass called a "waist?"
A. Because you could easily fit another pair of tits there.

* * * *

Georgie is walking down the street after a sex-change operation has transformed him into a beautiful woman. An old friend sees him and says, "Georgie, you look great . . . you're beautiful!"
Georgie says, "Thanks . . . but holy Christ, did it hurt."
His friend asks, "When they cut open your chest and put in those implants?"
Georgie says, "No, that didn't really hurt."
His friend asks, "When they cut off your dick and dug out a vagina?"

Georgie says, "No, that didn't really hurt."

His friend asks, "Then what did hurt?"

Georgie says, "When the doctor drilled a fucking hole in my head and sucked out half my brain."

* * * *

A man rushes into his house and yells to his wife, "Martha, pack up your things. I just won the California lottery!"

Martha replies, "Shall I pack for warm weather or cold?"

The man responds, "I don't care. Just get the fuck out!"

* * * *

Some guys were hangin' out, shootin' the breeze, and the conversation turned to their kids.

One guy says, "I've got five sons. All over six feet tall. Damn good basketball team."

Another guy says, "Right on. I've got nine sons and every one of them can field and hit. Great baseball team."

Third guy chimes in with, "Way to go. I've got eleven sons. Strong as oxes, every one of 'em. Helluva football team."

Then they look at the fourth guy in the group. First guy asks, "Well, how about your kids?"

The fourth guy replies a little sheepishly, "I have eighteen daughters. Enough for a golf course."

* * * *

Q. How are women like parking spaces?

A. The best ones are taken, and the rest are handicapped.

* * * *

A couple had been married for several years when suddenly the wife decides she'd like to have breast implants. The husband says, "Now, honey, you know we can't afford that kind of thing right now."

"But I see you looking at other women," pleaded his wife, "and I want to be as attractive as they are to you."

Days go by and the wife keeps insisting she needs breast implants, despite the protests of her husband. Finally, the husband has had it. So he says to his wife, "Honey, I have an idea. Every day, about twice a day, wad up some toilet paper, then rub it between your breasts. Repeat it 3 or 4 times each time."

"You think that'll make my breasts larger!?" asked his wife.

"Why not?" says the husband, "It worked on your ass!"

* * * *

5,000 men were asked to complete a survey on what they liked best about oral sex:

3% liked the warmth

4% enjoyed the sensation

93% appreciated the silence.

* * * *

A man lost his ears in a hair-cutting accident. No plastic surgeon could offer him a solution. He heard of a very good one in Sweden, and went to him. The new surgeon examined him, thought a while, and said, "yes, I can put you right."

After the operation, bandages off, stitches out, he goes to his hotel. The morning after, in a rage, he calls his surgeon, and yells, "You swine, you gave me a woman's ears."

"Well, an ear is an ear. It makes no difference whether it is a man's or a woman's."

"You're wrong! I hear everything, but I don't understand a thing!"

* * * *

An ugly woman walks into a shop with her two kids. The shopkeeper asks "Are they twins?"

The woman says "No, he's 9 and she's 7. Why? Do you think they look alike?"

"No," he replies, "I just can't believe you got laid twice.

* * * *

It was April first when a young father went to the hospital to see his newborn son. Standing outside the glass partition, the nurse pointed to his baby son. The nurse smiled as she lifted the baby from its cot. She then strolled over to the table and bounced the baby's head on the timber. The father was horror-struck and his hands went up to the window. The nurse smiled at him and started to swing the baby by holding it by its penis and scrotum. The father was pounding frantically at the glass partition by this time. The nurse let go of the baby and with a sickening thud the baby went careering into the wall. Blood and guts went everywhere. The father took a runing jump at the glass partition. The nurse picked up the baby and tore it's arms off as the father went hurtling through the glass. He was foaming at the mouth when he faced the nurse.

She said, "April fools! He was dead already!"

* * * *

Q. What's the difference between spit and swallow?

A. 50 pounds of pressure on the back of her head.

* * * *

A man wanted to get married. He was having trouble choosing among three likely candidates. He gives each woman a present of $5,000 and watches to see what they do with the money.

The first does a total make over. She goes to a fancy beauty salon gets her hair done, new make up and buys several new outfits and dresses up very nicely for the man. She tells him that she has done this to be more attractive for him because she loves him so much. The man was impressed.

The second goes shopping to buy the man gifts. She gets him a new set of golf clubs, some new gizmos for his computer, and some expensive clothes. As she presents these gifts, she tells him that she has spent all the money on him because she loves him so much. Again, the man is impressed.

The third invests the money in the stock market. She earns several times the $5,000. She gives him back his $5,000 and reinvests the remainder in a joint account. She tells him that she wants to save for their future because she loves him so much. Obviously, the man was impressed.

The man thought for a long time about what each woman had done with the money he'd given her.

Then, he married the one with the biggest tits.

* * * *

An American woman, a British woman, and an Italian woman were having lunch. The American woman said, "I told my husband that I wasn't going to clean the house anymore. If he wanted it clean, he would have to do it himself. After the first day, I didn't see anything. The second day I didn't see anything. Then, on the third day, voila! My husband had cleaned the whole house!"

The British woman agreed. "I told my husband that I wasn't going to do the laundry anymore. If he wanted it done he would have to do it himself. After the first day, I didn't see anything. The second day, I didn't see anything. Then, on the third day, voila! My husband had done both his and my laundry!"

The Italian woman chimed in, "I told my husband that I wasn't going to cook anymore. If he wanted home cooking he would have to either go by his mother's or cook for himself. After the first day, I didn't see anything. The second day, I didn't see anything. Then, on the third day, I began to see a little out of my left eye."

* * * *

These two guys walk into a bar, and they've each got a black eye. The bartender asks the first guy. "What happened to you?"

The guy responds "I had a slight mishap of words with my wife. You see, we were getting plane tickets, and the lady behind the terminal was REALLY good looking. When I accidentally said 'Two pickets to tits-burg' instead of 'Two tickets to Pittsburgh,' the wife hit me."

The bartender looks at the second guy and asks. "And you?"

The guy responds "I had a slight mishap of words also. This morning, while I was eating breakfast, I meant to say 'Please pass the margarine,' but instead I accidentally said 'You stupid bitch, you ruined my life'..."

* * * *

A blonde goes into a laundry mat and asks to have her sweater cleaned. The laundromat attendant doesn't hear her correctly and says, "Come again?"

The blonde blushes slightly and giggles, "Oh no, it's just mustard this time."

* * * *

What are the three reasons that make anal sex better than vaginal sex? It's warmer, it's tighter, and it's more degrading to the woman.

* * * *

Q. What do you call a sorority girl with a runny nose?
A. Full.

* * * *

There is more money being spent on breast implants and Viagra today than on Alzheimer's research. This means that by 2040, there should be a large elderly population with perky boobs and huge erections and absolutely no recollection of what to do with them.

* * * *

Three engineering students were gathered together discussing the possible designers of the human body. One said, "It was a mechanical engineer. Just look at all the joints." Another said, "No, it was an electrical engineer. The nervous system has many thousands of electrical connections." The last said, "Actually it was a civil engineer. "Who else would run a toxic waste pipeline through a recreational area?"

* * * *

A tour bus driver is driving with a bus full of seniors down a highway when he is tapped on his shoulder by a little old lady. She offers him a handful of peanuts, which he gratefully munches up.

After about 15 minutes, she taps him on his shoulder again and she hands him another handful of peanuts. She repeats this gesture about five more times.

When she is about to hand him another batch again he asks the little old lady why they don't eat the peanuts themselves. "We can't chew them because we've no teeth," she replied.

The puzzled driver asks, "Why do you buy them then?"

The old lady replied, "We just love the chocolate around them."

JOKE ANALYSIS
BY DR. BROWN

After a lecture a small mid-western college during which I may have inadvertently represented myself as more desirous of female companionship than a "hermit with a pair of Kate Beckinsale's panties on his head," I was being consoled by a concerned young woman. Obviously jealous of the attention I was receiving, we were interrupted by a "Hot Topic" surf punk named Jinx, who thought he would enhance the moment with this pithy tidbit;

Q. Why do women fake orgasms?
A. Because they think men care.

A funny joke, indeed, Jinx, playing as it does on the traditional sex roles of men as uncaring brutish animals.

But let me assure my female readership that this is far from the case with this author. No, no. To this joke professor, the act of lovemaking is an intimate encounter with the holy; a woman's pleasure is a sacrament to be lovingly cherished.

Indeed, nothing brings me greater fulfillment than showering a beautiful woman (although here I am perhaps being redundant, since all women possess an inner beauty that cannot be denied - especially some of the fat ones) with finery, then massaging her with sandalwood oils in a canopied wrought-iron bed surrounded by the flicker of cinnamon candles.

So I would shower you, dear reader, with rose petals as Enya played softly in the room. Then, ever so gently would I undress you, kissing you over every inch of your body. My soft voice would caress your most erotic organ, your mind, until you were transported to a higher realm, leaving our airport-adjacent motel far behind.

I would slowly press open the most intimate folds of your body, and lower my mouth onto you. I would tease you mercilessly, my tongue darting back and forth as you mewled in delight, bringing you ever closer to satisfaction, yet cruelly denying you release, your eager body now filled with lust-greed, arching back longingly against my maddening ministrations. Rest assured, my love, your Indian would be knocked out of his canoe.

Then, in accordance with your wishes, I would slip my thumb tenderly into your delicate rosebud, holding it there as you became accustomed to its opposable fullness.

Only then would I permit you your first orgasm. I would hold you tightly as a great rush of ecstasy blossomed from deep inside like some lush flower opening from the very center of your soul. You would find immeasurable comfort in my embrace, knowing that I would never allow any harm to ever come to you. Nor would I succumb to my desire to say "Thar she blows!" nor "Heyyyyyy now!" nor "Gesundheit!"

And then I would jerk off on your tits and get the hell out of there.

Coming in 2006 from

NATIONAL
LAMP☺☺N ®
PRESS

Why waste your time reading blogs of boring people? An imprisoned dictator has so much more to say.

A hilarious collection of parodies of magazines in a magazine format. What could be harder to explain?

Also coming this fall,

A brand new collection of True Facts
Funny-but-true. Absurd-but-true. Disturbing-but-true. They're all here.

Favorite Cartoons of the 21st Century
A brand new collection of cartoons from the next generation of cartoonists.

National Lampoon's Not Fit For Print
All the stuff that's too vile and too tasteless for us to publish anywhere else. Guaranteed to offend.